MW00477766

Lessons

FROM THE

Gridiron

by
R. McKenzie Fisher

New Leaf Press

First printing: August 1995
Second printing: April 1996

ISBN: 0-89221-298-5
Library of Congress: 95-69894

Cover by Multnomah Graphics, Portland, Oregon
Photo on page 16 courtesy of the Dallas Cowboys
Photo in page 42 courtesy of Tim Umphrey
Photos on pages 61 and 87 courtesy of the University of Illinois
Photo on page 76 courtesy of the University of Michigan
Photo on page 99 courtesy of Notre Dame University

All Scripture references, unless otherwise indicated are taken from the Holy Bible, New International Version, copyright 1973, 1978, 1984 by International Bible Society. Used by permission of Zondervan Publishing House.

Presented to:

_____

Presented by:

_____

Date:

_____

Dedication

There are those whose love and support afford anyone who writes the encouragement to do her/his best. The following people are those without whom this book would not have been completed:

My family — Mom, Ed, and Brian for always "being there" for me, and my brother Roger for his football days that began my interest in the game.

The Emmaus community — where I received the peace ("pax") and confirmation to write. (My Emmaus cross with its "Christ is counting on you" is always around my neck whenever I am writing as a reminder that I have a Co-Author.)

My church family at Trinity — for the pastors' wisdom and the support of my Sunday school class.

The staff at New Leaf who gave me the support I needed during this "quick write" book for football.

As always, Jesus, whose love brings fullness and joy to my life.

Foreword

Making a connection is obviously the object of every tight end and his quarterback. The most important connection I've made, however, is not one thrown by Steve Young. It is the connection to God I made when I accepted Jesus Christ as my Saviour several years ago. That relationship connects me to Christians around the world and from biblical times to eternity.

Jeff Brantley, relief ace for the Cincinnati Reds, and I made such a connection when he used to pitch for the San Francisco Giants. We worked on several community benefits for the youth in the Bay area. So, when Jeff wrote the Foreword for the book *Lessons from the Diamond* and then suggested I do the same for the football book, I knew this was something worthwhile. Author Rita Fisher made another connection through 49er chaplain Pat Ritchie, a good friend and mentor in Christ.

I've played the game of football since I was a kid and yet there were stories in *Lessons from the Gridiron* that were new even to me. I thoroughly enjoyed all of the trivia and history Rita shares, but the way she connects the everyday aspects of the game to our spiritual lives is really refreshing.

This book is written for men and women, sons and daughters, coaches and spectators. You don't have to understand every nuance of the game to be a football fan. Rita encourages everyone to find ways of enjoying this game. Better yet, she encourages everyone to find the real joy in life of knowing Jesus.

I also like the idea of peewee or Pop Warner coaches perhaps sharing these devotions with their teams before each game. Youngsters can learn a few facts and basics of the game, some great stats about current and former players, and most importantly, about God's love for them. Older sports enthusiasts and those involved with groups like Athletes in Action and Fellowship of Christian Athletes will enjoy a new perspective on the game they already love.

In "It's All about Timing," Rita talks about being either a primary or secondary receiver. I certainly understand that concept. As the primary receiver, the thrill of scoring a touchdown is awesome. But I also know that it is equally important (and just as exciting) to be the back-up receiver in case Jerry Rice is covered and Steve Young needs to pass elsewhere.

That's what I feel like in writing this Foreword — a secondary receiver. Rita may have written this book, but it is still a way for me to reach out to others in sharing the love of Christ. Fortunately, Rita (like myself) recognizes that Jesus is and should be the primary person in all our lives. May He richly bless you as you enjoy *Lessons from the Gridiron!*

Brent Jones

Introduction

When you're in third grade and your only brother, whom you adore, plays high school football, you learn the game of football. The fact that I was a girl didn't make any difference. I was a tomboy and enjoyed learning to throw a spiral. That talent later came in handy in MYF (Methodist Youth Fellowship) when we played touch football on Sunday afternoons and at weekend retreats. My passing reputation would be the topic of more than one classmate who wrote in our high school yearbook.

I enjoyed cheerleading at Williamsburg High and riding with the team to the away games (NOT a fun bus ride home when we lost). I didn't try out my senior year because I wanted to attend as a fan so I could watch the entire game (cheerleaders spend most of the time with their backs to the action).

In college I connived a way to get good seats to most of the Miami (Ohio) Redskins' games. First semester I joined "Block M," whose seats were between the 40 and 50 yard lines. We flipped formation cards during cheers and at halftime. Sophomore year I lived in the "jock quad" so I could get invited to the game by a varsity athlete since the varsity club had 50-yard-line seats. I was off-campus my junior year (working for the National Republican Committee during the 1968 presidential election). By my senior year I knew enough campus and political VIPs that I was usually invited to sit with one of them in the box seats near mid-field. (I did manage to study while on campus and received my degree in education.)

As a first-year teacher at the junior high level, I surprised my students by performing at a pep rally. If you've never heard the old Andy Griffith comedy routine, "What It Was Was Football," try to locate an old book of monologues. Put me in a pair of tattered blue jean shorts, tie my hair in pigtails, and paint some freckles on my face, and I can still drawl my southern accent and recite it. "I finally figured out that the object of this here game was to grab that punkin and run down the field without either getting knocked down or steppin' in something!"

Actually, I'm now more interested in sharing not just the funny side of football but facts and trivia about the game. More importantly, I want to tie these to our spiritual lives in hopes that men (and their wives and children) can enjoy the game from a new perspective.

When you're through with (or while you're reading) this devotional, I also challenge you to read the Book of Proverbs which has far more wisdom than any of our "Lessons" series. Because the Book of Proverbs has 31 chapters, my personal way of studying it down through the years has been to look at the date on the calendar and read the corresponding chapter. If I miss a day or two (or even a month or more), rather than feeling guilty, I just check the date and read that chapter's verses. Over the years I have read them all, but they never grow old. God seems to match the date with what is happening in my life at that very moment. I pray He will do the same for you.

In His love,
Rita McKenzie Fisher

Lesson 1
Pass Masters

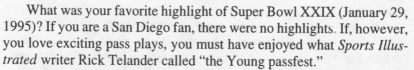

What was your favorite highlight of Super Bowl XXIX (January 29, 1995)? If you are a San Diego fan, there were no highlights. If, however, you love exciting pass plays, you must have enjoyed what *Sports Illustrated* writer Rick Telander called "the Young passfest."

Using only 1:24 in their first possession, Steve Young marched the 49ers downfield in three plays and threw a 44-yard touchdown pass to Jerry Rice. Their second possession took 1:53 and was capped by a 51-yard pass to Ricky Watters.

Young threw four more touchdowns and was the game's Most Valuable Player. Having held the highest quarterback rating in the league for four consecutive years, Young proved himself worthy to be considered one of the best ever in the game.

Telander said Young "effectively exorcised the Joe Montana ghost that had been haunting him for years." Young's predecessor in San Francisco, Montana had held the single-game records with five TD passes in Super Bowl XXIV.

What does it take to be a successful passer? It's a combination that involves knowledge of the plays and running patterns, the vision to see the field and locate open receivers, and the ability to throw the football correctly with the proper strength and accuracy.

What goes into the actual passing motion itself? In *Play Football the*

9

NFL Way, Tom Bass tells us the four elements:

(1) The *set* is "the last step in the quarterback's drop-back." The QB stops his backward momentum and plants his feet to begin the arm motion.

(2) The *forward step* shifts the QB's direction. "As his leg moves forward, the toe of the foot should be placed so that it aims directly at the quarterback's target."

(3) The *delivery* or *release* is the "critical stage." The "hips of the player should open up and be square with the target area." He should throw the ball with "the trunk of his body and not merely his arm," Bass warns. "A player who throws only with his arm and not his body, usually is inaccurate and loses velocity on the ball."

(4) The *follow through.* After releasing the ball, the passing arm continues its forward movement with the forearm coming over the top of the elbow and extending toward the receiver.

Finding a true relationship with God is much like these stages of the proper passing motion.

We must first stop the backward momentum. Until we realize we are sinners, we will not *set* our lives in order. Prison ministry leader Chuck Colson believes we must first be convicted by the Holy Spirit that we are indeed sinners. He says, "We preach about a new birth without mentioning the death of the old self first. What brings about the death of the old self is the awareness of sin."

Next comes the *forward step.* We must move in God's direction. While some services offer altar calls for people to literally "come forward," we can obviously come to Christ anywhere because He is everywhere.

He *delivered* us from our sins but we must "open up" and "be square" with God. With sincerity and honesty, we repent of our sins. We also put our whole body into these efforts — releasing ourselves mentally, physically, emotionally, and spiritually.

Finally, we must make the commitment to *follow through*. There should be a change in our heart and in our lives. Our actions and attitudes will now reflect His love and spirit.

Have you completed a personal acceptance of Christ as your Saviour? It will be unbelievable!

"Repent, then, and turn to God, so that your sins may be wiped out, that times of refreshing may come from the Lord" (Acts 3:19).

"Is this great or what? I mean, I haven't thrown six touchdowns in a game in my life. Then I throw six in the Super Bowl. Unbelievable." — Steve Young (after Super Bowl XXIX)

Lesson 2
"Hey, Coach!"

Which college football coach stands out in your mind as the best? Joe Namath would undoubtedly say "Bear Bryant." Troy Aikman might respond "Barry Switzer." (They were together at Oklahoma before Aikman transferred to UCLA.)

One coach, however, transformed collegiate football perhaps more than any other. When Knute Rockne came to Notre Dame as a student, he was already five years older than the other players. He didn't make the team the first year but was named captain his junior and senior years. He and quarterback Gus Dorias developed a new way to throw the football (the spiral), new formations, and innovative plays. Much of the modern passing game began with this duo and their new coach, Jesse Harper.

After Rockne graduated magna cum laude, Harper hired "Rock" as his assistant. Four years later Rockne became head coach.

Some of Rockne's Irish stars would help him further revolutionize the game. He originally spotted George Gipp drop-kicking a ball on campus and encouraged him to join the team. Gipp would drop-kick (not place-kick) a 62-yard field goal to beat Western Michigan his first year on the team. He would also become the team's quarterback and one of Notre Dame's leading runners of that era. During Gipp's junior year (1919 — Rockne's second as head coach) Notre Dame went undefeated and was ranked first in the nation.

Shortly after the senior football banquet, Gipp lay dying of pneumonia in a local hospital. Telling Coach Rockne he was not afraid to die, he then uttered the now famous line: "Someday, Rock, when things on the field are going against us, tell the boys . . . go out there and win one for the Gipper." Rockne supposedly saved the challenge for the 1928 Army game. With an 0-0 tie at halftime, that line motivated the Irish to a 12-6 victory.

Rockne also coached the famed "Four Horsemen," whose combined skills in the backfield led him to develop the "Notre Dame Shift" — a varied play off the T-formation.

In addition to his ability to add new excitement to the game with his innovative plays, Rockne's other strength as a coach was communication. He explained new concepts so his players understood. If need be, he was willing to get down on the field himself and demonstrate as an example. He knew when to speak and when to wait. (Who else would have held "Win one for the Gipper" for eight years before using it?) Rockne worked well with his players and assistants in communicating what needed to be done to win. In 13 years as coach at Notre Dame, his record was 112-12-5! He left a legacy that challenged all Irish coaches of the future.

Communication is still key in effective coaching. At the professional level, some assistants are in the booth high above the field during the game so they see "the larger picture." They communicate with other coaches on the sidelines via headphones. The defensive coordinator talks with his unit as soon as they come off the field, while the offensive coaches are next to the head coach, helping call the plays. While this may seem confusing, they all still report to the head coach. He is in control.

Prayer is much the same. While life is often chaotic, prayer is simply communicating with God. He sees the larger picture. He also sent Jesus to earth as our example. While God may get input from others who are praying for us, He puts it all together with the best plan for our lives. Put Him in control.

He is our Head Coach.

"Then Jesus told his disciples a parable to show them that they should always pray and not give up" (Luke 18:1).

"He was a football coach and athletic director of Notre Dame . . . in the words of Christ, 'Thou shalt love thy neighbor as thyself' . . . I think that he supremely loved his neighbor." [part of Knute Rockne's eulogy] — Father Hugh O'Donnell (President of Notre Dame)

Lesson 3
The Play Book

"One of the smartest quarterbacks in the game, Boomer Esiason, said it took him two-and-a-half years to master the Cincinnati offense when he came out of college" (*Sports Illustrated*).

Even though players who reach the pro level are already familiar with the basics found in all team play books, most NFL teams spend regular time in the classroom. Chalkboards, diagrams, films, and question and answer sessions are all a part of the weekly schedule. Then it's out of the drawing room and onto the field to practice execution.

The NFL coach with the most career wins (327 as of 1/29/95), Don Shula, knows the routine. "If our players are worrying about assignments, they have a tendency to hold back," says Shula. "They should be so familiar with . . . the play book, that when the games start, they're operating on auto-pilot — the way you do when you drive a car. You don't think about what your hands and feet should be doing — just do it!"

One of the quickest students in the NFL is Bernie Kosar. Released from the Cleveland Browns after the 1993 season had begun, he was picked up by Dallas. A week earlier, quarterback Troy Aikman had suffered a hamstring pull that sidelined him. Taking a crash course in the Cowboy play book, Kosar learned 67 plays in one week. Cowboy offensive coordinator Norv Turner was amazed and impressed, "He had

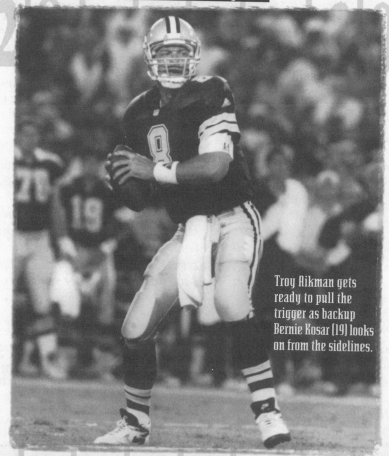

Troy Aikman
Dallas Cowboys

Troy Aikman gets ready to pull the trigger as backup Bernie Kosar (19) looks on from the sidelines.

to know who his primary, secondary, and tertiary receivers were on every passing play and how many yards each receiver was going to run on each play." Plus, the numbering system for calling plays was new to Kosar.

"Kosar learned the nuts and bolts of the Dallas attack in three days." Then he led the Cowboys to a 20-15 win over Phoenix. "His numbers for the day: 13 completions in 21 attempts for 199 yards with no interceptions and the touchdown pass to [Jay] Norvacek."

Kosar obviously understood that talent and experience without knowing the plays won't make it in professional football. He studied and learned well.

We all study and learn in our daily lives. We attend seminars to develop more efficient ways of running our business. We read articles to find out which car to buy. We watch the news to learn what's happening in our communities and around the world.

We study what we hope will help us discover ways to live fuller, more effective lives. Are we as intentional about learning new ways to make our spiritual lives fuller and more effective?

First we need to read God's Word. Using study guides such as Barclay's commentaries is an excellent way to better understand the Bible. Other outstanding Christian authors offer us overwhelming options in good reading — from the self-help books of the Minirth-Meier clinic to the fiction of Joseph Girzone's *Joshua* series.

Then as we read the newspaper, magazines, and other secular materials, we can balance them against what we learn from our Scripture-based studies.

Our goal in studying is not just taking in knowledge. That is being "**in**formed." It is not going along with everything we read — being "**con**formed." It is not changing our opinions just for the sake of change — being "**re**formed." Our goal as Christians is to take all we learn through God's mind to become "**trans**formed" into what He wants us to be.

Rather than merely being in-formed about God, we want to be formed-in His likeness!

"Do not conform any longer to the pattern of this world, but be transformed by the renewing of your mind" (Rom.12:2).

"We take 28 pages of tests every week. When we get out there on Sunday, we know what we're doing." — Dewey Selmon (former All-Pro LB, Tampa Bay)

Lesson 4
Hand-Offs

Some of the most exciting plays in football are the twisting, dodging, scampering, and darting of the running backs as they avoid blocks and tackles to advance the ball — maybe even dashing all the way into the end zone for a touchdown.

Detroit Lion Barry Sanders is "shifty, quick, and explosive — claiming the title as pro football's best current back with the fourth-highest season rushing total ever (1,883 yards) in 1994." The only running backs with higher season totals are: Eric Dickerson (2,105) in 1984, O.J. Simpson (2,003) in 1973, and Earl Campbell (1,934) in 1980. Playing college ball at Oklahoma State, Sanders won the 1988 Heisman trophy. Little surprise, he set collegiate single-season records: most points (234 on 39 TDs) and yards gained (2,628). As Sanders stretches his professional stats and yards gained in the Silver Dome, Detroit fans have nicknamed him the "Silver Stretch."

His counterpart for the Dallas Cowboys, Emmitt Smith, has set some records of his own. Named the MVP of Super Bowl XXVIII in 1994, Smith carried the ball 30 times for 132 yards and scored two touchdowns. He had led the NFC in total yards rushing the previous three years (1991-93). The only other pro backs to lead the NFL (not just their conference) in rushing yards for three consecutive years were: Cleveland's Jim Brown (1963-65) and Houston's Earl Campbell (four years, 1978-81). Chicago's

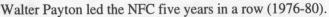

Walter Payton led the NFC five years in a row (1976-80).

Sanders and Smith have made "carrying the ball" an art form. However, before they can streak for touchdowns or rush for records, they must first master the art of the smooth hand-off. Working together with their respective quarterbacks for a successful transition is vital. The field commanders, as quarterbacks are sometimes called, must be willing to let go of the ball in hand-offs and passes in order to accomplish the mutual goal of scoring touchdowns and winning games.

Often in our lives, we are not willing to "let go." For those in leadership roles, this means learning to delegate. Too many times we try to "do it all by ourselves." Why is that? It's been said, "If you want something done well, do it yourself." However, that sometimes means "if you want it done *your way*"! Perhaps we don't let go at times because we don't want someone else to get the credit. Share the work means share the glory! Is that why we don't let go?

Maybe we're afraid they will have a better idea and show us up. It's beginning to sound like our ego might be trying to pull a "quarterback sneak." It's become a competition with the old win-lose scenario.

We need to play by the rules of Denis Waitley's book, *The Double Win*. He believes the win-lose game gets us "hooked on power." Power doesn't always spell success. "Success" for Waitley "must become a two-way street." It simply means your success becomes my success. "If I help you win, I win, too!"

We need to build these win-win situations in business, family life, coaching peewee football, church work, and all areas of our lives. We have to "hand-off" in order to allow others to do their

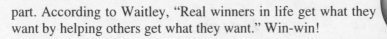

part. According to Waitley, "Real winners in life get what they want by helping others get what they want." Win-win!

"Now the body is not made up of one part but of many. . . . The eye cannot say to the hand, 'I don't need you!' And the head cannot say to the feet, 'I don't need you!' " (1 Cor. 12:14, 21).

"I don't know if Earl Campbell is in a class by himself, but it sure don't take long to call the roll." — Bum Phillips (Oilers Coach, 1978)

Lesson 5

The Kicking Game

Are you familiar with the Peanuts cartoon where Lucy holds the football for Charlie Brown, only to yank it away at the last second, causing him to fall flat on his duff? Poor Charlie will never kick a field goal!

Do you know who holds the record for the longest field goal in NFL history? Tom Dempsey kicked one 63 yards for New Orleans (vs. Detroit) in 1970. The place-kicker with the most field goals is Jan Stenerud. In 19 years with the Chiefs, Packers, and Vikings, he successfully punched the pigskin across the goalpost 373 times.

The record for most total points scored by any individual (at any position) in NFL history is also held by a place-kicker. In his 26-year career (also a record), George Blanda scored 2,002 points while playing with the Bears, Colts, Oilers, and Raiders. While he played several positions, including quarterback, he only scored nine touchdowns during his tenure in the game. Over half his points were on field goals — 335 to be exact, for 1,005 points. Conversion kicks accounted for the remaining 943 points.

In 1950 in their rookie year as a team, the Cleveland Browns won the NFL Championship Game (pre-Super Bowl) on a 16-yard field goal by Lou Groza with 28 seconds left in the game to beat the Rams, 30-28.

The Giants won the NFC play-off game to go to the 1991 Super

Bowl (XXV) by scoring only field goals against the 49ers. New York's Matt Bahr kicked five field goals to win the game, 15-13.

Also in 1991, the longest game in NFL history ended with a field goal. After 82 minutes and 40 seconds (on Christmas Day, no less), Garo Yepremian booted the pigskin through the Dolphin goalpost to beat Kansas City, 27-24.

Place-kickers are careful in choosing a holder with good hands who can receive the long snap from the center. No one wants a "Lucy." Often, the back-up quarterback is the holder. Most teams discourage their starting QB from holding since there is risk of injury. Some teams select a wide receiver or running back who is used to catching the ball.

After taking the snap, the holder must spin the ball so the laces face the target. If the laces are to the side, it will cause the ball to wobble and lose accuracy. If the laces are toward the kicker, it will cause a loss of power and distance. The ball also needs to be on a predetermined spot, positioned for the kicker's style, and held with a light touch. Matt Bahr prefers the ball tilted back and slightly to the right to slow down his natural "hook." Jeff Hostetler was most often the holder for Bahr when they both played for the Giants.

There must be a great deal of confidence between the kicker and his holder. If the holder does not do his job properly, the kicker cannot get the accuracy and distance he needs to the goal. If the kicker is not careful and accurate with his kick, the holder's hands could be injured. The place-kicker and holder have a great deal of trust in one another.

Who do you trust in your daily life? Is there someone you can count on to "hold the ball" for you?

We all need friends — those individuals with whom we feel comfortable enough that we can trust them with our deepest secrets. They are people whose opinions we respect if we need advice or another perspective on some problem.

In *The Book of Virtues,* William Bennett says that friendship goes beyond acquaintances and affection. We usually share common interests and often similar goals in life. True friendship calls "for frankness, for self-revelation, for taking friends' criticism as seriously as their expressions of admiration or praise, for stand-by-me loyalty, and for assistance to the point of self-sacrifice."

Do you have such a friend? Are you such a friend?

"A friend loves at all times, and a brother is born for adversity" (Prov. 17: 17).

"Kicking the ball really isn't playing. You're out there for a few seconds and you're a hero." — George Blanda (Hall of Fame, 1981)

Lesson 6
Monday Night Football

"Congratulations! You've been selected the MVP," the locker room broadcaster informs the star-of-the-game. "To what do you attribute your outstanding play this afternoon?"

"I want to thank Jesus for the ability He has given me and also my teammates who gave me a lot of support," the athlete responds. "I couldn't have done this alone."

The next probing question will either delve into the other players' roles or some co-analysis of highlight footage. The follow-up question will **not** be about the player's relationship with Christ.

Frank Gifford, Al Michaels, and Dan Dierdorf may talk about a player's shoe contract or restaurant and his college career. If a player has had a run-in with the law, we hear about that as well. It would be wonderful to also hear the *Monday Night Football* crew discuss a player's involvement in Fellowship of Christian Athletes or the projects he supports due to his religious commitment!

"If network news was your sole source of information, you would have to conclude that religion is all but non-existent in America today," says L. Brett Bozell III of the Media Research Center.

Print journalism doesn't fair much better. *Sports Illustrated* found it "unreal" when Colorado football coach Bill McCartney retired to devote time to his wife and Promise Keepers, a Christian men's support group he co-founded. How could he walk away from "a $350,000-per-year contract with 10 years remaining? To spend time with his wife and his god?" (By the way, there is no small "g" in McCartney's God!)

Nowhere in the article do we learn that Promise Keepers encourage men to remain faithful to their wives, provide financial (as well as emotional) support for their families, get involved in their churches and communities, and commit to reaching out in unity to other races and denominations.

In the summer of 1994, Peter Jennings hired evangelical reporter Peggy Wehmeyer for *World News Tonight*. Rather than going for the extremist point of view on religious issues, Jennings said, "There's a need to cover people who connect their faith to their everyday decisions."

TV Guide reporter Peter Ross Range says many journalists think "religion is mostly a private affair, not a proper topic of public discourse." Yet, they cover celebrity and political extra-marital affairs. What could be more private than that?

Before we criticize the media too heavily, we need to take a look at our own daily broadcast messages. One local minister says, "Christianity is personal but not private." Michael Vilardo shares that we must each make the decision to receive Christ as our Saviour. "No one else can make that decision for us. That makes it personal. But it is not to be private. We are to reach out to others and share what Christ means to us."

"Unfortunately, many people get the idea that witnessing for Christ means standing on the corner yelling at passersby, or obnoxiously breaking into people's conversations at inappropriate times and with a judgmental spirit and know-it-all attitude," says Jay Kesler, president of Taylor University (Indiana). Having led Youth for Christ for many years, Kesler understands "it is vital that we avoid taking a holier-than-thou approach."

Simply put, "witnessing" means sharing with others what Christ has done for us. It is sharing how prayer, reading the Bible, and having Christian friends to lean on makes our decisions wiser and more successful. It also means sharing times of defeat when we did not listen to God's spirit or the suggestions of faithful friends. The more we allow Christ into our daily lives, the more we will have to share.

How much of your daily play-by-play includes Jesus?

"With that same spirit of faith we also believe and therefore speak. . . . so that the grace that is reaching more and more people may cause thanksgiving to overflow to the glory of God" (2 Cor. 4:13, 15).

"Pro football might be mankind's most highly publicized human endeavor." — David Hill (President, Sports Division, Fox network)

Lesson 7
Rivalries

Who was your high school rival? Do you cringe when you see teams wearing the colors of your old high school opponent? One high school graduate wouldn't even consider a college that was interested in him because he didn't think he could wear a green and yellow uniform — he would feel like a traitor.

Perhaps college football has produced the most intense and long-term rivals. Any game with a Big Ten team playing a Pac-Ten team is a precursor to the Rose Bowl. Similar rivalries have been created by new postseason games with invitations extended to specific conference champions. The most intense confrontations, however, remain inside conferences: Ohio State vs. Michigan, Arizona vs. ASU, Alabama vs. Auburn, Nebraska vs. Oklahoma, USC vs. UCLA.

Non-conference-related rivalries do exist. Notre Dame seems to evoke a "let's kill them" attitude from all of their opponents. Whether it's another Hoosier team like Purdue or cross-country rivals like Boston College or Florida State, the Irish seem to bring out the best in their opponents. Army vs. Navy and West Point vs. the Air Force Academy are military battles played out on the gridiron.

One of the oldest rivalries in the nation is between DePauw and Wabash in Division III. Separated by only 27 miles of flat Indiana backroads, these two schools celebrated their 100th classic in 1993 with complete game-day coverage by ESPN-2 and a full-spread in *Sports Illustrated*. The Monon Railroad ran between Greencastle (DePauw) and Crawfordsville (Wabash) in the early years. A 350-pound brass bell from one of the line's locomotives is now painted half red (Wabash Little Giants wear red and white) and half gold (DePauw Tigers uniforms are black and gold). The Monon Bell is awarded annually to the team that wins the contest on the gridiron. The game that happens in between is "Who can steal the bell?" Nearly any DePauw or Wabash fan will tell you, "It's every student's obligation to study hard, to be honest and forthright, and to try to steal the Monon Bell."

Rivalries always produce a "higher level" of play and importance. You can lose an entire season but beat your rival in the final game and you have been redeemed. The opposite is also true. While going to the Rose Bowl is the goal, losing "the big one" against Michigan still puts a damper on an Ohio State season.

Satan tries to throw a "wet blanket" on our spirits as well if we're not careful. He is our true rival and will use whatever he can to defeat us.

All we need to do is read the headlines about the crimes and other atrocities taking place in society. Even then, many blame racism, poverty, lack of family support, and other more innocuous "demons." We do need to work at eradicating these problems but we must recognize the devil at work.

Unfortunately people refuse to see evil for what it is. Following the Oklahoma City bombing in April 1995, syndicated columnist Cal Thomas warned, "Acknowledging the existence of evil — not just evil people but evil itself — is a prerequisite to understanding and controlling it."

Thomas fears that we will continue to look with abhorrence at these horrible events around us only momentarily. Then we move back into our own comfort zones of indifference. Thomas says, "Denying that evil exists, and it is a proper metaphor for the worst kind of behavior, ensures that evil will prosper."

To defeat evil, **we** must become its rival. To defeat Satan, we must depend on God and do His work on earth.

"Do not be overcome by evil, but overcome evil with good" (Rom. 12:21).

"We can't lose to these people!" — Oklahoma quarterback Steve Davis, before a 1975 game with in-state rival Oklahoma State

Lesson 8
Offsides

The official throws his flag. Can you "make the call"? What infraction of the rules took place? On which team? How many yards will the penalty be?

Understanding the basic rules will help you better enjoy the game.

Interference is probably the most controversial infraction the official has to call. It is a judgment as to whether the defender is truly going for the ball and whether any other bumping or shoving takes place before the receiver touches the ball. If interference is called, the offense gets the ball at the point of contact, often a first down. There is also offensive interference, where the receiver actually bumps or shoves off the defender, who also has a right to try to catch the ball (15 yards against the offense).

Holding is the illegal use of a player's hands to detain another player instead of blocking or tackling (10-yard penalty for offensive holding; 15 for defensive holding).

Clipping is when a player blocks or tackles a player from behind once he crosses the line of scrimmage (15-yard penalty).

Roughing the kicker is called if the defense makes contact with the placekicker or punter while he is in the motion of kicking. They may block the ball but not the punter. Conversely, the defense is not permitted to bump or tackle the quarterback unless he still has the ball. Once he releases the ball, it is considered *roughing the passer*. A *late hit* penalty is similar. If a player is hit after he is down or already out-of-bounds, the defense can be called for a penalty. (All of these penalties are 5 yards.)

Illegal procedure is called when the offense has fewer than seven players on the line of scrimmage or if an offensive player moves forward before the ball is snapped. It is also called when either team has more than 11 players on the field (5-yard penalty).

Delay of game can be called if the offense takes more than 30 seconds between plays (5-yard penalty).

The most often called 5-yard penalty is *offsides*. This is when any defender crosses over any part of the line of scrimmage before the ball is snapped. Quarterbacks will often change their tone of voice before calling the final snap number in hopes of drawing an opponent offside.

"They blew the call! How could he be standing three yards from the interference, looking straight at the players involved, and NOT call THAT penalty?" Have you heard similar complaints during a coach's post-game interview? It's always easy to blame the referee.

Following in his dad's tradition, Dave Shula, head Cincinnati Bengal coach, seldom, if ever, places blame on the officials. Even in a close game, he will always meet the press with the same response, "If we had played a better game, we wouldn't get ourselves in a close enough situation that one or even two bad calls means the difference between winning and losing." We all should be so personally accountable for our actions.

 In his book, *If Only*, David Seamands says we have become a nation of mental disorders to blame for every crime. People blame their parents for not loving them enough or loving them too much.

They count shyness or being too talkative as handicaps and disorders. Everyone makes "an attempt to explain away personal responsibility for sinful behavior," says Seamands.

People "claim victimization as the reason for *who* and *what* they were, and *how* they were living out their lives." There are indeed some victims — those "suffering people who had no choice in, control over, or responsibility for what happened to them." However, at some point, we each must decide to take control. We must put the past behind us, get help if necessary, and break the cycle of dysfunction within our lives and the lives of our families.

As TV pastor Robert Schuller says: "Don't fix the blame. Fix the problem."

"No temptation has seized you except what is common to man. And God is faithful; he will not let you be tempted beyond what you can bear" (1 Cor. 10:13).

"Once a game is over, as far as Don [Shula] is concerned, it's over. I've never seen a quote from him in the paper saying the officials lost the game." — Art Holst (NFL Referee)

Lesson 9
It's All in the Timing!

The following duets all have it. Steve Young and Jerry Rice; John Elway and Shannon Sharpe; Brett Favre and Sterling Sharpe; Jim McMahon and Cris Carter; Terry Bradshaw and Lynn Swann; Joe Namath and Don Maynard. The list is endless, but can you guess what they all share?

Timing! That near-perfect timing that is necessary for successful quarterbacks and their favorite receivers. Without it, your game plan might as well forget any pass plays.

Fox TV analyst and former coach John Madden says the quarterback has to adjust his timing to the pattern. If it's a short pass, you can't waste time dropping back too many steps. On longer passes, you need more time to set up so the quarterback must get further back in the pocket. "If a QB is throwing a medium-range pass with his wide receivers cutting at 15 yards downfield, it doesn't make sense for him to be ready to throw the ball before his receivers are ready to catch it," says Madden. "It's all timing."

Don Maynard (former NFL wide receiver) talks about working with Joe Namath while with the Jets. "Right from the first when we'd miss on a pass we'd get back together and discuss it right away. What happened? Was I early or were you late, or what?" explained Maynard of their strategy. "We didn't want to carry bad feelings around even for two or three plays." Maynard says they also "played a lot of catch." They worked on one pattern so often that they actually tried running it with Namath blindfolded in practice. How did they do? Recalls Maynard, "We tried it one day and hit four out of five and the fifth one I just did touch." That's timing! In the 1968 AFC Championship game they connected for two touchdowns, six passes, and 188 yards gained. The final score was a 27-23 victory over the Raiders.

Another aspect of the timing involves both the primary and secondary receivers. The quarterback needs to keep both in his line of vision and at least look toward one and then the other. Some quarterbacks who suffer several incompletions per game may be looking only toward their primary receivers, which becomes a sign to the defense where to rush. Good quarterbacks always look off-target to confuse the defense. It is also to his own benefit in case the primary target cannot get open, he can then more easily adjust his timing to locate and hit the secondary receiver. It is the receiver's responsibility to get open, but there are times when the defense has a good read on the play and it isn't possible. That's why the secondary receivers are necessary on every call.

Are we open so God can look our way and count on us to be one of His receivers on every call? As a primary receiver, if we are not open to His direction, He may need to pass some job or talent on to someone else. The opportunities work both ways. Are we willing to be secondary receivers? Just because we are not "asked first" to fill some position in the church is no reason to turn down the role. That is being too sensitive — to the degree of being pride-filled rather than Spirit-filled. God needs both primary and secondary leaders to carry out His game plan.

His timing is always impeccable. Often miracles might be explainable in human terms but it is in their timing that we see the unexplainable. There are also times when what may seem like a failure to us becomes an opportunity for success in God's timing.

Will you be open and available when the time comes that He calls on you?

"Humble yourselves, therefore, under God's mighty hand, that he may lift you up in due time" (1 Pet. 5:6).

"I have to read the defense even as the QB is doing . . . and we both have to do it right. Needless to say, it takes practice to get the timing between us just right." — Don Maynard (Hall of Fame, 1987)

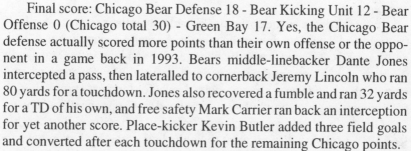

Lesson 10
The Big "D"

Final score: Chicago Bear Defense 18 - Bear Kicking Unit 12 - Bear Offense 0 (Chicago total 30) - Green Bay 17. Yes, the Chicago Bear defense actually scored more points than their own offense or the opponent in a game back in 1993. Bears middle-linebacker Dante Jones intercepted a pass, then lateralled to cornerback Jeremy Lincoln who ran 80 yards for a touchdown. Jones also recovered a fumble and ran 32 yards for a TD of his own, and free safety Mark Carrier ran back an interception for yet another score. Place-kicker Kevin Butler added three field goals and converted after each touchdown for the remaining Chicago points.

Former Bear coach Mike Ditka was a believer in tough defense. He once asked linebacker Mike Singletary, "When's the last time you broke a helmet?" When Singletary replied it had been a while, Ditka challenged him, "I want to hear one break." While playing at Baylor University, Singletary broke 16 helmets, "all of them his own." Rick Telander, *Sports Illustrated* columnist, confirmed the story with Baylor's publicist who said the entire team usually only broke two or three a year.

Telander says, "Pain is the thing that separates linebackers from everyone else on the field — both dishing it out and receiving it." Yet Telander says many defensive giants have a "Jekyll and Hyde nature . . . off the field they generally keep cool; on the field they explode."

Exploding on the opponent's offense is the job of the defense. The three basic defensive attacks are: zone, man-to-man, and prevent. In all three, the defensive line blocks any holes the offense might try to open, either causing a tackle or at least a detour for the runner with the ball. The linebackers' responsibility is to charge the QB or tackle the oncoming running back. The highlight of a game for any linebacker is to "sack the quarterback!"

In a zone defense, the cornerbacks each cover their respective side of the field and the safety covers the middle. As man-to-man suggests, each cornerback is assigned a specific wide receiver and the safety stays with the tight end. A prevent defense is normally used late in a game when a team is ahead and uses extra defensive backs for long pass protection — to "prevent" any long bombs being completed to the opponent's receivers.

Obviously, the respective players' roles overlap at times. Pittsburgh's Rod Woodson says "If you want to be the best cornerback, you have to play like a linebacker, too. You have to take on pulling guards and tackles, and you must hit tight ends and running backs." Perhaps his intensity explains why he has proven one of the best in the NFL. "You can't be passive. If you don't sell out on every play, you'll come up a play or two short."

As Christians, we can't be passive either. We can take a lesson from the three types of football defense.

Our zone defense is relying on other Christians for support and advice. Being a part of a Christian family is a real bonus. Developing close Christian friendships, attending a Bible-believing church, and getting involved in that fellowship are a part of our spiritual zone.

Man-to-man is that one-on-one time that we must spend with

God alone. Take time each day to have devotions — to read the Bible and to talk with, and listen to, Him.

A prevent defense is needed when difficult days are ahead or a potential temptation arises. For instance, if there is the temptation for sexual misconduct, avoid intimate situations (including movies with explicit scenes). Double date. Spend time with your family playing games or only go out where there is a crowd. Find similar precautions when it comes to temptations with alcohol, drugs, and other challenges of daily life.

At times it may take all three methods of spiritual defense. We don't want to come up short!

"But if anyone does sin, we have one who speaks to the Father in our defense — Jesus Christ, the Righteous One" (1 John 2:1).

"Trench play, that area of the battle between two lines of antagonistic football teams, is a game of its own within a football game." — Reggie White (Defensive lineman, All-Pro 10 times, All-Pro MVP 1986)

Lesson 11

Super Sunday

Over 40,000 seats remained unsold at Memorial Coliseum in Los Angeles on January 15, 1967, for Super Bowl I. The NFL Green Bay Packers beat AFL entry Kansas City 35-10 in a rather lackluster event. The Packers would also win Super Bowl II over the Raiders 33-14, but this time at least to a full house in Miami the following January.

Super Bowl Sunday has changed! While more than 75,000 packed Joe Robbie Stadium in Miami for Super Bowl XXIX in 1995, the "Super Bowl as sport is eclipsed by the Super Bowl as spectacle," says *TV Guide*.

It is the most hyped television event each year. There's the "Pre-Game Report," then the "Countdown to Kick-off," followed by "The Kickoff," "The Halftime Report," and the "Post-Game Wrap-Up" — all bearing advertising sponsors. ABC television used 27 cameras, 50 microphones, and 20 miles of cable to cover Super Bowl XXIX in 1995. Estimated viewership was 135 million in the USA with 750 million worldwide.

Where are all of these fans the rest of the year? What is it about this one Sunday that draws so many people?

The same could be said of Easter Sunday! Why is it that our churches are overflowing on that one Sunday of the year? Most congregations are squeezed elbow-to-elbow in pews that normally have plenty of space. Many set up extra chairs in the aisles and some even hold additional services for the celebration of Christ's resurrection. If we really care about Christ, where are we the other 51 Sundays of the year?

Those who never miss a Sunday or worship service should be commended. Many of them believe that to do anything **other** than church or family activities on Sunday is a sin. They do not eat out, go shopping, travel, or involve themselves in any form of commercialism on Sunday. They point to the fourth commandment about keeping the Sabbath as a holy day. Hopefully, however, they do not point fingers and judge others who might not share their opinions.

It is a somewhat confusing and sometimes controversial issue. In the Old Testament the Sabbath was Saturday. Nowhere in Scripture does that change. Still, we should not criticize those who do choose to incorporate the Old Testament laws into their modern lives.

We can take a lesson from S. Truett Cathy, owner of Chick-fil-A. He refuses to open his fast food chain on Sunday as his way of honoring God. His restaurants, most located in shopping malls that are open on Sundays, continue to flourish as well as those restaurants doing business that day. He does not condemn the mall owners nor judge the other restaurateurs, but he sticks to his own convictions.

When challenged about His disciples gleaning food from a field on the Sabbath (and His own healing ministry as well), Jesus himself expressed that God made the Sabbath as a day of rest for us. It is for our own good, but Christ scolded the Pharisees for their rigidity in keeping Old Testament law. As far as our setting aside a special day to worship God, Christ brought the message that we need to worship Him every minute of every day.

How do professional players, who for the most part play their games on Sunday, find time for worship services? When is their day of rest? Pre-game Football Chapel is available each week, and most teams take off either Monday or Tuesday from regular practice schedules.

Regardless of our personal viewpoints about Sunday games, eating out, and other activities for the day, we do need to attend worship service more than once a year. Where will you be next Sunday?

"Then he [Jesus] said to them, 'The Sabbath was made for man, not man for the Sabbath' " (Mark 2:27).

"The Super Bowl is like the last chapter of a hair-raising mystery. No one would think of missing it." — Pete Rozelle (former NFL Commissioner)

Mike Singletary
Chicago Bears

A wild-eyed and ferocious middle linebacker, Singletary had a reputation for breaking helmets and opponents' hearts during a Hall of Fame career with Chicago.

Lesson 12
Huddle Time

What goes on in the huddle? It's more than just calling numbers and colors. It's making sure everyone is going to run the same play.

Former NY Jet Joe Namath says the quarterback has to take control. "We're out there in the huddle and a receiver will say, 'I can beat this guy,' and somebody else on the line will say, 'Just run it over here, Joe,' and that can get to be a hassle sometimes." The quarterback can't make everyone happy. Namath firmly believes you must have confidence in all your teammates, but he says, "I'm the quarterback and I have to make decisions based on what is soundest at the moment." He not only called the shots but the outcome of Super Bowl III when he brashly told the press the Jets were going to defeat the Baltimore Colts. "I guarantee it," read the sports headlines earlier in the week. The final score on January 12, 1969? Jets 16, Colts 7.

In the late 1930s the Washington Redskins ran one of the more interesting plays called the "Befuddle Huddle." On the kick-off return, only three men stayed on the line. Meanwhile the other eight players ran to where the football landed. They "huddled momentarily and then broke in different directions, each hunched over as if he had the football." Part of the play's success depended on everyone running about the same speed. Anyone "breaking away" would be recognized as the true carrier. The play became obsolete when the NFL started requiring five men on the line of scrimmage for kick-offs.

Often in daily life our families must feel like the coverage team in the "Befuddle Huddle." We are all so busy running in so many different directions that we hardly know what each other is doing.

Pulitzer Prize-winning columnist William Raspberry reports that most Sunday morning worship services in our churches have more women than men in attendance. He says this is not due to the feminist movement but rather to "male abandonment." He is encouraged, however, in what he sees as a "trend the other way."

Colorado football coach Bill McCartney and some friends decided back in 1990 that men in particular needed to take more responsibility within their families. Approximately 60 men began to "huddle together" in prayer. The response was the Promise Keeper movement that has exploded. In one year 4,200 men showed up for the first conference; 22,000 came the next year. By 1993 more than 50,000 men filled CU's football stadium. In 1994 seven conferences were held and the next year 13 stadiums and auditoriums around the nation were sold out.

Raspberry was impressed "that 52,000 men packed [Washington, DC's] RFK Stadium (and paid $55 each for the privilege) in a declaration of religious renewal . . . that hopes to bring men back to church — and back to Christian responsibility."

The Astrodome, Silverdome, Georgia Stadium, Mile-High Stadium, Hoosier Dome, LA Coliseum, Kingdome, and others all sold-out, which translates into more than half a million men coming not to see football games but to learn to stand as men of faith in their families and communities.

They will go home with the challenge to begin men's groups in their local churches — to support one another and to hold each other accountable in their Christian walk. Their primary goal is to serve Christ and to build "huddle time" with their wives and children.

"A football team that seldom huddled wouldn't make it to the Dust Bowl, let alone the Super Bowl," says Ron Hutchcraft of Youth for Christ. "In the same way, a husband and wife must protect their regular huddle — no matter how busy they are." In looking at his own early marriage, Hutchcraft said, "I saw how many days slipped through our hands without touching each others' hearts. Many days we have been around each other, but not *with* each other."

Energize your family with some huddle time tonight!

"Each one of you also must love his wife as he loves himself, and the wife must respect her husband" (Eph. 5:33).

"Some of his contemporaries have stronger arms, and several possess a more delicate touch, but no player energizes a huddle better than [Boomer] Esiason." — Tim Sullivan (sports columnist for the *Cincinnati Enquirer*)

Lesson 13

Concentrate

"The Catch!" "The Immaculate Reception!" "The Hail Mary!" "The Miracle Catch!" All are popular headlines on the sports pages or sport magazines whenever a bedazzling end-zone pass reception scores the winning touchdown. You can probably think of several of those games yourself.

In *NFL Top 40* alone, there are three such stories. "The Catch" (1/10/82) was Joe Montana to Dwight Clark for San Francisco over Dallas, 28-27. "The Immaculate Reception" (12/23/72) was Terry Bradshaw to Franco Harris and Pittsburgh over Oakland, 13-7. Roger Staubach threw "The Hail Mary!" to Drew Pearson (12/28/75) for the Dallas win over Minnesota, 17-14.

Then there was the famed Boston College "Hail Mary" over Miami. Or was it Colorado's "Hail Mary Catch" shocking Michigan? And there must be a Notre Dame "Hail Mary!" over some opponent!

Sports Illustrated did a special anniversary issue with "40 Pictures to Remember." There was MVP Lynn Swann catching one of his four touchdown passes from Terry Bradshaw against the Cowboys in Super Bowl X.

A photo layout of outstanding Super Bowl catches would not be complete without at least one shot of Steve Young to Jerry Rice in Super Bowl XXIX. Rice concluded a record-breaking year by taking over Jim Brown's (126) career touchdown receptions. Rice ended the 1994-95 season with 138 lifetime professional TD completions. He had his ninth season with 1,000 yards or more and set all sorts of Super Bowl records.

What does it take to make those spectacular catches? Knowing your route patterns, timing with the quarterback, out-maneuvering the cornerbacks and safeties, and good hands. Speed for the final burst to the end zone is helpful as well. But ask the receivers and they will give you one word: concentration.

Reggie White, who knows more about sacking the quarterback to cut off the pass before it starts, wrote a book for touch football fans. Even in it, he says, "All your concentration must be on the football. Follow the ball all the way into your hands." says White. Then he emphasizes, "NEVER TAKE YOUR EYES OFF THE BALL!"

We also need that emphasis of intense focus and concentration in our spiritual lives. "Focused attention" is one definition for meditation that is a valuable method of personal worship. Meditation requires our listening more and talking less than conversational prayer, which should also include listening. Otherwise, it would be a monologue.

Many people think of something like transcendental philosophy when we mention meditation. Richard Foster, in his classic book *Celebration of Discipline,* says that Eastern meditation is an attempt to empty the mind, but Christian meditation empties the mind in order to fill it with God's thoughts! "**De**tachment is the goal of Eastern meditation; whereas Christian meditation goes on to a richer, fuller **at**tachment to Christ and to other human beings," says Foster.

For meditation, we need to get away from the distractions. It may be in our homes or while taking a walk. It may be sitting on our back porch with a cup of early Saturday morning coffee. Can you hear the birds chirping? Smell the lilacs in bloom? Breathe in the fresh air and God's love. Exhale the stress and worries of the office and other problems. Reading some Scripture will prepare your heart for this time alone with God. That is simple meditation — time alone with Him.

Don't think that only men of biblical times were meditators. Foster also says, "God spoke to them not because they had some special abilities, but because they were willing to listen."

Are we willing to listen to Him?

"May my meditation be pleasing to him, as I rejoice in the Lord" (Ps. 104:34).

"Concentration is all-important. And the key is to concentrate your way through the bad times." — Dan Fouts (former Charger QB, Hall of Fame, 1993)

Lesson 14

The Referee

He usually stands somewhere behind the offensive backfield and has the same authority over the actions on the gridiron as does a judge in the courtroom. The referee is in charge of all other officials.

His crew for a professional game normally consists of six other officials. The umpire stands behind the defensive line and calls all violations in that area of action. The head linesman (at one end of the line of scrimmage) is responsible for tracking the forward progress of the ball. He keeps track of the downs and the yardage needed for a first down and works with the sideline chain crew. The line judge (at the other end of the line of scrimmage) watches for line violations and is the official time keeper in the game. The field judge (behind the defensive secondary) watches for infractions on downfield plays and punts. The back judge (toward the sidelines behind the defensive line) is responsible to catch foul play by the backs and receivers. The NFL also uses a side judge similar to the back judge to assist with calls from the opposite side of the field.

One real-life judge actually played the game of football. Drafted by the professional Pittsburgh team, Byron R. White was the highest paid rookie ($15,000) in the NFL in 1938. He had earned All-American status at Colorado and was known as "Whizzer." White played professional ball only long enough to save money to attend Yale Law School (he graduated in 1946). He was appointed as a Supreme Court Justice in 1962.

We sometimes like to appoint ourselves as judge — often questioning at least one of the referees' calls. Unfortunately, we also seem to enjoy making judgments in other areas of life.

In his book, *Moments for Fathers*, pastor Robert Strand shares a wonderful story about a Supreme Court judge in England. Three mission churches came together to worship with their "mother" church on a particular Sunday. Kneeling at the altar rail was a former thief now released from prison, saved through Jesus, and committed to the church. Kneeling beside him was the same judge who had sent the burglar to jail for seven years. Later exclaiming, "What a miracle of grace!" the judge was not referring to the ex-convict. Having come from a life of crime, the criminal saw a better life with Christ. That was not difficult to understand.

"I went to Oxford, earned my degrees . . . and eventually became a judge," said the Supreme Court Judge. He went on, "Nothing but the grace of God could have caused me to admit that I was a sinner on a level with that burglar." We are **all** on that same level.

"For in the same way you judge others, you will be judged, and with the measure you use, it will be measured to you" (Matt. 7:2).

"Like me? I don't know. It would be nice if people didn't always judge me without understanding me." — Michael Irvin (All-Pro receiver for Dallas)

Lesson 15

Who's on Crutches?

Check the sideline of any football game and you will most likely find at least one player on crutches. If you've watched much football, you will see why. More than one violent injury has been re-played in slow motion until we wince in pain ourselves as we witness the "snap" of a bone. Maybe you remember the hit NY Giant Frank Gifford took back in 1960 that rendered him unconscious until after he was carried into the locker room. He suffered a serious concussion with side effects that kept him out of the game for over a year. Who can forget Redskin Joe Theismann's fractured leg that eventually ended his career in 1985? If you saw Raider Napoleon McCallum's knee being severely crushed in a game at the beginning of the 1994 season, you won't be surprised if he has to call it quits as well.

Just reading about injuries makes one's spine shiver. In 1992, Eagle Randall Cunningham "tore the medial collateral and posterior cruciate ligaments in his left ankle." The same year Steeler Bubby Brister "had an Achilles tendon from a cadaver transplanted into the knee to replace a ruptured posterior cruciate ligament."

Being sidelined, for those who love to play the game, is a painful experience. MVP of Super Bowl XXI, New York Giant Phil Simms was injured for the team's repeat performance in 1991. "I felt so out of place. I couldn't do anything except hobble around on those stupid crutches," said Simms.

Lineman Brad Benson later helped Simms realize that the Giants would not have made it to the play-offs without his regular season leadership. Still, after Super Bowl XXV was over, Simms said, "I was glad the Giants won, but I felt no satisfaction. I couldn't help thinking how great it would have been to be a part of it all."

It's not easy being on "crutches" — whether the injury is physical or perhaps emotional. When we don't have the energy or the determination to overcome our problems, we may find some "crutch" to give our life meaning.

To some it is their position, a title, money, a fancy home and car, "things," education, good works, and maybe "who you know." What gives your life meaning? In listing these "possible crutches," retreat pastor John Keeney challenged us to consider, "Whatever is our *prop* becomes our god."

There are times when we need to lean on others for support — but only temporarily, taking long enough to heal. If it becomes long-term and overly dependent, we may avoid dealing with some major issue. We cannot expect others to do for us what we are not willing to do for ourselves.

We also need to allow others to lean on us — but again only for the short haul. Permitting too much dependency makes us an "enabler" and is not healthy for either party concerned. We need to be careful not to "bear so much of the other's burden that he gets to continue with his unproductive behaviors" and make the problem worse (*Serenity Meditations*).

Whatever you do, don't coerce a friend into being an unnecessary "crutch" for you. By all means, share openly and ask for help, but don't tie their hands. It is most unfair to tell a friend, "You are the **only** person I can count on and you can't tell **anyone** else."

Don't let anyone put you in this position either. Hold their names privately but seek outside advice if you need it to better help them. We can keep confidences and concerns un-named but seek the wisdom of others.

The only true "prop" we have is God. Our best resource is to help others find His support.

"I pray that you may enjoy good health and that all may go well with you, even as your soul is getting along well" (3 John 1:2).

"A player is used to dealing with pain. The tough part for me is knowing what pain is good and what pain is bad. I don't want to set the elbow back, but I don't want to be not working it hard enough to get ready." — Joe Montana (after tendon reattachment in his arm in 1992)

Lesson 16

Winning Is Everything

"Winning isn't the most important thing, it's the only thing," is the famous quote by Vince Lombardi. While not the winningest coach in NFL history, Lombardi coached the Green Bay Packers to victories in both Super Bowls I & II (1967-68). That record might have been more impressive as the Packers won the (pre-Super Bowl) NFL championship three more times during the nine years he coached Green Bay (1961, 1962, 1965). He also coached the Washington Redskins for a single season. Inducted into the Hall of Fame in 1971, the Super Bowl trophy is now named in his honor.

Lombardi was well known for being hard-nosed and demanding. He expected (and received near) excellence from his players. "No one is perfect, but boys, making the effort to be perfect is what life is all about," insisted Lombardi.

The only team to have a perfect season was the Miami Dolphins at 17-0 in 1972.

Lombardi's theme carries into life, "If you'll not settle for anything less than the best, you will be amazed at what you can do with your lives."

Another former football great with a similar attitude is Jim Brown (nine Pro-Bowls and Hall of Fame inductee in 1971). As one of the game's greatest running backs of all time with the Cleveland Browns, he says, "Success is there for those who want it, plan for it, and take action to achieve it." He has carried that theme from the gridiron to the ghetto and in-between. After his retirement, he served as a consultant with the Browns counseling players about life in and out of football.

In 1987, Brown started the Amer-I-Can program to help kids in gangs become productive members of society. He finds serious-minded youngsters and involves them in "a 60-hour curriculum aimed at building self-esteem and a feeling of empowerment." When they finish the program, Brown locates jobs for them in security firms and sporting-goods management.

Brown challenges other leading professional athletes to follow suit. "If I had the participation of the top 20 athletes in this country," said Brown, "we could probably create a nationwide gang truce."

What a welcome relief for the inner cities of our nation! In addition to athletes and other leaders, the church needs to be active within these communities. What are we doing to set a higher standard — looking toward a Lombardi-like "perfection"? As long as we believe there are no solutions and are willing to remain uninvolved, life on the streets will continue to be a war zone.

In his book, *You Can!,* Dr. Frank Minirth reminds us that Satan and society constantly wage an invisible war attacking our morals and values. Dr. Minirth gives hope: "Recognize that defeat happens because we're in a war, one that we will ultimately win."

This does not mean as Christians we will go undefeated. The more we try to serve God, the harder the devil will try to throw up any roadblock, any negative thought that he can to get us to turn our backs on Christ.

This idea brings new insights and new incentives. We can now feel, "If Satan is fighting me this hard, I must be doing something important!" Our God is stronger and more powerful. As we see defeat as an opportunity to rely on God for victory, we can handle even losses that come our way.

We aren't perfect. We will make mistakes. We will have failures. But, we can learn from our failures how better to prepare for the next round of battle. God has the only perfect game plan for guaranteed victory in the end!

What has God taught you through past failures? What are you learning that can help Him win the ultimate battle?

"For everyone born of God overcomes the world. This is the victory that has overcome the world, even our faith. Who is it that overcomes the world? Only he who believes that Jesus is the Son of God" (1 John 5:4-5)

"Winning isn't everything but it beats the heck out of losing. . . . You can never be perfect in football, but perfection is what we strive for." — Mike Ditka (former Bears coach, Hall of Fame, 1982)

Lesson 17

On the Line

It's rare that the offensive line gets any publicity — unless it's negative. Statistics are unfair in this regard. Quarterbacks, receivers, running backs, and kick-returners get the most publicity with the glory of touchdowns. Place-kickers make the news on winning field goals. Cornerbacks, safeties, and other defensive players can even intercept a pass to score.

The defense gets credited with sacks, pressures, strips, forced fumbles, recovered fumbles, etc. The only stat the offensive line might have is: zero — to all of the above. Paul Zimmerman, *Sports Illustrated* columnist, says "A sack brings a crowd to its feet. A standoff, which is really a victory for the offensive lineman, is a ho-hummer."

"What gets me," says Art Shell, (former player and head coach for the LA Raiders) "is that a guy gets a sack and he's jumping up and down. What about the 38 or 39 times out of 40 pass plays that he gets blocked? If a tackle did all that jumping up and down, he'd never make it through the first quarter."

The basic job of the offensive line is to protect the quarterback and open a hole for the running backs. If they don't, you can be assured they will get some press — bad press.

"Offensive linemen are the foundation of your whole team," according to John Madden, one of the more popular television analysts. "An offensive lineman has to be thoughtful (or smart), whereas a defensive player is more animalistic." The defense reacts to what is happening on the field, but the offensive line must know every component of each play being called so they can keep a wall of protection between the on-coming defense and the quarterback. This is especially true of the left tackles.

"What does my left tackle mean to me? Only life or death," says Steeler quarterback Mike Tomczak. Numerous quarterbacks have made the Pro Hall of Fame but to date only seven offensive tackles. One of those is Art Shell, whom many consider the best left tackle to ever play the game. A close second might be Anthony Munoz who was All-Pro 11 years in a row from the Bengals. Said Sam Wyche, Munoz's coach when both were in Cincinnati, "He'd be out there in bad weather at lunchtime. . . . Other guys were catching a little nap, but there was nothing but pride in the way Anthony prepared himself — and played."

Sports Illustrated's NFL '94 Preview issue featured photographs of some of the current offensive giants in an article entitled "In The Line of Fire": Gary Zimmerman (Denver), John Jackson (Pittsburgh), Richmond Webb (Miami), Harris Barton and Steve Wallace (San Francisco), Jim Lachey (Washington), and Lomas Brown (Detroit), with a separate article about Indianapolis Colt Will Wolford. The preview also mentioned high expectations for first-round draft rookies: Bernie Williams (Eagles), Wayne Gandy (Rams) and Todd Steussie (Vikings), and second-round draftee Marcus Spears (Bears). They and other offensive linemen are the unseen and unsung heroes of the game.

Within our churches there are unseen heroes and heroines as well. The faithful praying members of our congregations (often the senior citizens or shut-ins) are as, if not more, important than our speakers in the pulpit. Sending a note to someone who is ill is equally meaningful (sometimes more) as teaching a Sunday school class. Taking groceries or a meal to a shut-in is as much a Christian witness as writing a devotional book.

What unseen challenge is God laying on your heart at this moment?

"Be careful not to do your 'acts of righteousness' before men, to be seen by them . . . so that your giving may be in secret. Then your Father, who sees what is done in secret, will reward you" (Matt. 6:1,4).

"The NFL is like an amusement park. You go in, ride the merry-go-round, have fun and then, sooner or later, it will be over. . . . Right now, I'm enjoying the ride." — Richmond Webb (All-Pro Dolphin offensive tackle)

Lesson 18

Nicknames

"Politically correct" nicknames are in the news. Only schools like Alabama's Crimson Tide may be safe from protests.

Miami University teams (Oxford, Ohio), known as the Redskins since 1928, became embroiled in the conflict. The school had a long and trusted relationship with the official tribe of Miami. Their position did not oppose the term Redskins as long as it was used with respect. The mascot logo was a masculine and accurate painting of a Native American, not a cartoon caricature. The tribe furnished the clothing and regalia for the live mascot, Chief Miami (changed from Hiawabop in the 1970s), and the student selected for the role was trained in the authentic tribal dances. Still, activists protested. So, in 1994 Miami President Paul Risser announced that all newly formed teams would henceforth be called "the Tribe." Current teams could maintain the original nickname unless they desired to change. Even that did not appease extremists, but the Oklahoma-based Miami tribe issued a statement supporting the new name. They had requested early in the change process that some symbolism between the University and the tribe persist.

Interestingly, Jim Thorpe, perhaps the most gifted professional athlete of all time, was five-eighths Native American and his grandfather was the famed Chief Black Hawk. Yet Thorpe did not seem to be offended by such issues as team nicknames. He even played

Harold "Red" Grange
University of Illinois

part of his football career for both the Cleveland Indians in 1921 and the Oorang Indians, a team he also coached in 1922-23 in the newly formed NFL. The Oorang team fielded only players of Native American decent, but the name Oorang was not of Indian origin but the name of a breed of champion Airdale dogs the team owner wanted to promote.

While it may have been most apt, Thorpe's Indian name, "Wa-tho-huck" nor its meaning "Bright Path," was ever used as a nickname for the gifted athlete. Other football players' nicknames, however, are perhaps better known than their given names.

Do you know the real names of the following stars? Bubba Smith, Hacksaw Reynolds, Boomer Esiason, "the Snake," Ickey Woods, Deacon Jones, the Galloping Ghost (check bottom of next page for the answers). Other nicknames are more descriptive of personality or ability: Broadway Joe Namath, (Billy) White Shoes Johnson, "Refrigerator" (or the Fridge" for short) Perry, Mean Joe Green, Dandy Don Meredith.

As with many nicknames, the "Four Horsemen" received their famed title from a local sportswriter, Grantland Rice. Did you know that these Notre Dame greats also had individual nicknames? Famine, Pestilence, Death, and Destruction! Respectively, by position and given names they were: QB Harry Stuhldreher, HB Don Miller, FB Elmer Layden, and HB Jim Crowley. Current ESPN anchorman Chris Berman is famous for thinking of a moniker to match almost any athlete.

From whom did Jesus get His many names? The prophet Isaiah foretold us Jesus would be known as "Wonderful Counselor, Mighty God, Everlasting Father, the Prince of Peace" (Isa. 9:6). Jesus gave us nicknames of himself that describe our relationships with Him. He is: "the Bread of Life" (our sustenance) (John 6:35), "the Light of the World" (to shine in the dark world of sin) (John 8:12), "the Good Shepherd" (to lead and protect us) (John 10:11, 14), and "the resurrection and life" (the Easter story) (John 11:25). He also tells us that only through Him as the "gate" can we reach God and eternity (John 10:7, 9). He is "the way, truth, and life" (John 14:6). As the "vine," He wants us to be branches, tied to Him for life itself (John 15:1, 5). Only through our dependence on Him can we bear the fruit of good works. (Also see John 1:29,34; 3:16.)

What do you call Jesus?

"Therefore God exalted him to the highest place and gave him the name that is above every name, that at the name of Jesus every knee should bow, in heaven and on earth and under the earth, and every tongue confess that Jesus Christ is Lord" (Phil. 2:9-11).

"Arrogant, pompous, obnoxious, vain, cruel, verbose, a showoff. I have been called all of these. Of course, I am." — Howard Cosell (Monday Night Football, 14 years)

Nicknames: Charles Smith, Jack Reynolds, Norman Esiason, Ken "the Snake" Stabler, Elbert Woods, David Jones, Red "the Galloping Ghost" Grange.

Lesson 19
Pride vs. Confidence

Standing over an opponent he just sacked, the linebacker points his finger at the flattened quarterback and dances a jig. On a similar sack, a different linebacker gives a teammate a "high five," signifying a job well done. Both actions are seen on the field every week in high school, college, or professional football. Probably in peewee games, too, since the kids mimic what they see older players doing.

Arrogance or confidence? The latter player certainly shows better sportsmanship!

The confidence of the quarterback is a key factor in the success of any team. When a QB passes the ball, there are basically three possibilities: a completion, an incompletion, or an interception. That's why his confidence is crucial. The quarterback can't lose confidence in himself or his receivers and blockers on an incompletion or interception. As a leader, he must let go of each play and move ahead to call the next play, believing in its success.

"Height and weight may vary considerably from one quarterback to another, but all successful quarterbacks have an inner strength and belief in themselves," says Tom Bass in his book, *Play Football the NFL Way*. They "bring an air of confidence to the field and the huddle that is quickly transmitted to the players" both offense and defense.

Former NFL coach John Madden agrees, "The more confident

a QB sounds in calling the play, the more confident his teammates will be in running that play."

According to Roger Staubach (former QB for the Cowboys 1969-79 and MVP of Super Bowl VI), the key to this confidence is being prepared. He says, "Confidence comes from hours, days, weeks, and years of constant work and dedication." Starring for the Naval Academy in college, Heisman winner in 1963, Staubach knew fully about such dedication. Upon graduation he had four years of naval duty he had to fulfill. He had to work out on his own and remain both physically fit and mentally and emotionally strong until he could enter the NFL. The Cowboys and Staubach were a perfect fit. Coach Tom Landry called every play and as a naval officer, Staubach was used to following orders — and giving them. He exuded confidence in the Cowboy huddle.

What is the difference between pride and confidence?

Pride is filled with self-centeredness and self-promotion — an egotistical "look at me" attitude. We can be proud of someone else, but when we keep focusing on ourselves, we become "I"dolizers.

A positive attitude about ourselves is essential. Self-respect and the belief in our abilities to do a good job, plus a lot of hard work, like Staubach says, will build confidence. But we should not leave out those who have helped us — parents, teammates, spouses, teachers, others, and especially God.

We have been created by God and in His image. All our talents are gifts from Him. "Christians should be encouraged to excellence and accomplishments for the glory of God," says Jay Kesler, president of Taylor University. He reminds us that even though Michelangelo may have been proud of his work in the Sistine Chapel, "When a person looks at the ceiling of that chapel, he is drawn toward God. He is inspired to worship God, not Michelangelo."

What are you doing to draw others to God? To whom do you point after a job well done?

"Being confident of this, that he who began a good work in you will carry it on to completion until the day of Christ Jesus" (Phil. 1:6).

"I'm ready. I'm completely ready. And I know I'm ready. That's confidence." — Roger Staubach (Hall of Fame, 1985)

Lesson 20

Conversions

Scoring in football is somewhat unique. In baseball you only score by crossing home plate. You can get various hits, walks, and combinations and you may even get four runs on a grand slam, but each run scores the same — one at a time across the plate. In basketball, you can hit a field goal for two points, toss in a three-pointer from behind the arc, or shoot a free throw for a solo point, but to count, the ball must go through the hoop each time.

In football, however, you can score several ways for varying point values. Running the ball or catching a pass in the end zone for a touchdown earns six points. The conversion after the TD is scored by either running or passing the ball again for two points or kicking it through the goalpost for a single point. Kicking a field goal is worth three points. Unlike other sports, the defense can actually score in football. They can intercept or recover a fumble to run for a touchdown but they can also score by tackling the opponent's ball carrier in their end zone for a safety and two points. Blocking a punt that goes out of the end zone is also a safety.

Can you remember a game where each type of score was the winning effort? Touchdowns win games all the time. It's not that unusual to watch a field goal float over the goalpost for a victory. In 1970 a Super Bowl was won for the first time by a field goal, when rookie kicker for the Baltimore Colts, Jim O'Brien, put one through the uprights from the 32-yard line with only five seconds on the clock. Colts 16 - Cowboys 13!

While you don't see many safeties, in an extremely close game those two points could mean the difference between winning and losing. Obviously the same thing can be said of the conversion after a touchdown.

A conversion is also the biggest decision we make in our spiritual lives. It is making a definitive decision about one's belief in and commitment to God. Luis Palau, an evangelist and author, says there are three basic steps.

Step one is admitting we have sinned. We may try to fool ourselves or others, but we know within our hearts that we are not where God wants us. Secondly, we must believe that Jesus is God's Son and that He died on the cross for us. Just as the football must go over the cross-bar of the goalpost in order for a field goal to count, we must look to the cross of Calvary for our conversion.

The final step is to seek forgiveness and accept Christ into our lives. Palau says, "This last step is a personal decision. It is an act of the will, for we can either reject or receive Christ." He warns, "Too many people depend on inherited, second-hand faith. But only authentic faith leads to life eternal."

Like football, there are many ways one can reach the goal. Some people feel the need to step forward and kneel at an altar of prayer. Others make this decision while reading their Bibles or a printed tract like those called "Four Spiritual Laws." Some may find the guidance or assistance of a minister or friend helpful in understanding the commitment they are making. Others meet God face-to-face through prayer and solitude. It may happen quietly in your pew at church, or you may

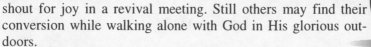

shout for joy in a revival meeting. Still others may find their conversion while walking alone with God in His glorious outdoors.

Our conversions may all be different, but however we come to Him, Christ is Saviour of us all!

[Jesus speaking] "I tell you the truth, whoever hears my word and believes him who sent me has eternal life and will not be condemned; he has crossed over from death to life" (John 5:24).

"A blocked-kick has been the difference between winning and losing an awful lot of football games." — George Allen (LA Rams coach — following a recovered kick that was run to the 5-yard-line, setting up the winning TD against the Packers on 12/9/67)

Lesson 21
Halftime

Halftime at football games provides a wide variety of entertainment whether you're at a Friday night high school game or the Super Bowl extravaganza.

In some areas of the country, the competition between the two high schools' marching bands may be as fierce as the football game itself. College units get into the spirit as well. The Ohio State Marching Band has a reputation of its own. Buckeye fans roar when the designated tuba player "dots the i" in their famous "script Ohio" formation. Alumni all over the nation jump to their feet in recognition of the *Notre Dame Victory March*, *On Wisconsin*, and other fight songs. USC's armored mascot rides horseback around the stadium after each Trojan touchdown.

Cheerleaders and drill or dance teams also provide halftime entertainment at all levels of football. The 1995 National High School Cheerleading Championships were broadcast by ESPN from the MGM Studios at Disney World. Paul Laurence Dunbar High School from Lexington, Kentucky, won the varsity division with Christian Brothers High School from Memphis, Tennessee, taking the co-ed category. With that win, CBHS had won 6 out of the past 10 years. In a similar competition from MGM-Disney, college cheerleaders from across the USA rallied. The University of Kentucky won the cheerleading contest; Louisville took first place in the dance team division. At the pro level, the Dallas Cowboy cheerleaders have produced pin-up calendars, entertained troops overseas with Bob Hope, and been the subject of a television movie.

Super Bowl halftime has become a spectacular event. Michael Jackson performed in 1993, and Travis Tritt, Tanya Tucker, and the Judds in 1994. Super Bowl XXIX was a 12-minute Disney-themed production on a 100-yard field with a cast of thousands. It was filled with stunts and special effects called "Indiana Jones Adventure: Temple of the Forbidden Eye."

Even the commercials running during the Super Bowl have become entertainment. *TV Guide* said, "When most people watch TV together, nobody talks except during the commercials. When people watch the Super Bowl, everybody talks *except* during commercials." One would expect the ads to be spectacular since the average 30-second spot running during the January 28, 1995, game cost $1 million. By comparison, a 30-second ad for Super Bowl IX cost $107,000.

Many ministers could fulfill their annual church budgets with the income from just one 1965 ad, let alone the current rate. When they "pass the plate" on Sunday morning, are we prepared to give our fair share?

Our worship services have our own version of halftime entertainment. We enjoy the choir, bell choir, children's choir, and other special music of the church. A sampling of favorite hymns are: "Joy to the World" and "When I Survey the Wondrous Cross" (by Isaac Watts), "Christ the Lord Is Risen Today" and "Jesus, Lover of My Soul" (by Charles Wesley), "Blessed Assurance" and "Rescue the Perishing" (by Fanny Crosby) and "Amazing Grace" (by John Newton). Many churches are offering a variety of folk music ("Lord, I Want to Be a Christian," "Jacob's Ladder," and "Go Tell It On the Mountain") and music by more modern song-writers like Bill and Gloria Gaither, Don Wyrtzen, Michael W. Smith, Amy Grant, and others. Are you humming your favorite song yet?

Many churches regularly use liturgy such as responsive readings and the Lord's Prayer. Expressive dance and drama are being added in many services today. All of these expressions, as well as the sacrament of Holy Communion, are meant to draw us closer to Christ and to give Him glory. There are many ways of sensing God's presence and praising Him.

How many of these are a part of your worship? Are there areas that might use your talent?

"He put a new song in my mouth, a hymn of praise to our God" (Ps. 40:3).

"Send a vol-ley, cheer on high, Shake down the thun-der from the sky. What tho' the odds be great or small, Old Not-re Dame will win o-ver all. While her loy-al sons are mar-ching On-ward to vic-tor-y." — last lines of the Notre Dame Victory March

Lesson 22

Fakes

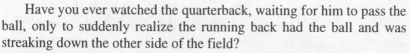

Have you ever watched the quarterback, waiting for him to pass the ball, only to suddenly realize the running back had the ball and was streaking down the other side of the field?

Most teams have several "fakes" in their play book. A quarterback fakes to a back, then tucks the ball away and dashes for yardage himself on what's called a "bootleg." The same fake followed by a drop back and pass is called a bootleg-pass or a play-action-pass. On a "draw" play, the QB drops back as if to pass and then as covertly as possible, hands off to a running back.

These hidden plays are devised to throw the defense into one pattern and then suddenly change, hoping they can't readjust quickly enough to stop the advance of the ball.

Everyone involved must act their part fully for the play to be successful. On a draw, the receivers must run patterns and act as if the ball is coming their way. Laying back or running nonchalantly will be a giveaway that the play is going to someone else. Likewise, the running back must carefully "protect" the "invisible" ball on a bootleg. If two steps into the fake, he shows he does not have the ball, the defense will still have time to sack the QB or re-focus on the wide receivers. The quarterback must also maintain his intention to pass the ball on a draw, or the defensive line will collapse on the running back.

Penn State's running back Ki-Jana Carter was the number one pick (taken by the Bengals) in the 1995 pro draft in April. At Penn State, the quarterback often forgot to carry out the fake, because "with Ki-Jana's explosiveness, I find myself just watching him. Then I get yelled at on Monday in meetings."

In the world around us we are constantly being fooled by "fakes" of another kind. The Bible warns us there will be "false prophets" and Satan does everything he can to trick us into believing in anything other than Christ. Paul and Silas were thrown in prison for calling a spirit of fortune-telling out of a slave girl who had been making money with the evil practice for her master (Acts 16:16-24). Other "masters" are making fortunes today by enticing those who are vulnerable.

You can't watch television, especially cable, without being inundated by advertisements and 900 phone numbers for various psychics, dinaetics, and other programs that do not rely on Christ. Don't be taken in by the popular celebrities who endorse these "readings" and such nonsense.

While many people see the above programs and most of the following as harmless, they can all be "traps" that quietly lead us into believing in something other than God and seeking advice from others instead of Him. Have you ever tried a Ouija board, tarot cards, having your palm read, or wearing crystals? How closely do you read your horoscope?

Cult leaders like David Koresh (Waco) and Jim Jones (Guyana) used Scripture to lure vulnerable individuals into their cults. How can you recognize such "false" prophets or cults?

Ask yourself the following questions (based partially on a Sunday school lesson by Dr. Melvin E. Dieter). Do they merely use the name of Jesus or **do they truly honor Him**? **Is salvation only through Christ** or by their own divine nature? Do they add "new revelations" from God or **do they rely on His Word as written? Are they open and honest** or exclusive and seclusive? **Is their loyalty to Jesus** or to the group leader? **Do they publicize financial statements** or keep records secret? Are the leader's views the only ones accepted or **can you read the Bible and pray out loud by yourself?**

If you cannot answer "Yes" to the **bold questions,** beware! We can't afford to be misled by false prophets. Don't let them fake you out!

"Do not be carried away by all kinds of strange teachings" (Heb. 13:9).

"If you don't stand for something, you will fall for anything. If you don't believe in Someone, you can be fooled by anybody." — sign on a church bulletin board

Lesson 23

Where's Your Center?

Can you name the two 1994 all-star centers chosen for the Pro-Bowl? If you can, you are among the minority of fans or you live in Texas. Mark Stepnoski of the Cowboys and Bruce Matthews of the Oilers were the All-Pro centers from the NFC and AFC respectively that year.

After five years in professional football, Stepnoski had been named All-Pro twice. In his first 12 years, Matthews was an All-Pro 7 years (1988-1994). His father, Clay Matthews, Sr. played for the 49ers in the 1950s and his brother, Clay Jr., was an All-Pro linebacker in 1985, 1987-89. Stepnoski is a graduate of Pitt; Matthews from USC.

A Michigan center earned his notoriety in another profession. Gerald Ford, 38th president, played center for the undefeated Wolverines in 1932 and 1933. Voted most valuable player of the 1934 team, he played on the college all-star team that lost to the Chicago Bears 5-0 in 1935. Ford was offered contracts by both the Detroit Lions and the Green Bay Packers but chose instead to become an assistant football coach at Yale from 1935-1938 until he entered law school there.

While other linemen can concentrate solely on their blocking positions, the center must first focus on correctly snapping the ball to begin each play. "Knowing he's going to get blasted as soon as he snaps the ball, a center needs more mental discipline than anybody at any other position," according to former coach and television analyst

Gerald Ford
University of Michigan

John Madden. The tendency might be to snap the ball a second early to get ready for the block, but Madden reminds us that can cause a fumble because the ball is not arriving properly in the quarterback's hands.

With the exception of the kick-offs, every play of the game begins with the center. He is a key player to the success of any team.

How we begin (our birth) and how we are "centered" are also keys to success in life. If we are born into loving families, we have a head start on positive self-esteem and a sense of belonging that psychologists today understand are important to mental and emotional health. If our families are Christians, our core or beliefs are even healthier.

Even if our "arrival" was not into a well-adjusted and loving family, there is hope. Dave Thomas, founder and familiar television personality for Wendy's restaurants, was born to an unwed mother in New Jersey. He was adopted by a couple in Michigan but his new mother died when he was only five. While he moved several times with his dad (to new jobs and through two marriages), his adopted grandmother — Minnie Sinclair — instilled a lot of his beliefs. Thomas has found that by sharing his story at seminars he touches others who find inspiration for their own non-traditional lives. He shares briefly of honesty and faith that go back to his early years with "Grandma Sinclair."

Gary Rosberg, founder and president of Family Legacy Christian Counseling, works with families in all sorts of crises. One of his statements brings hope to us all: "The family you came from is important, but not as important as the family you will leave behind."

If your birth family or your adopted family did not provide the love and support that you needed, what are you doing to make certain that does not happen to your own children? What are you doing to break any cycle of dysfunction?

Seek counseling if necessary. Take a parenting course. Join a church and Sunday school class and put Christ at the center of your life. Become a part of the "family of God."

"When I was a child, I talked like a child, I thought like a child, I reasoned like a child. When I became a man, I put childish ways behind me" (1 Cor. 13:11).

"A good center hangs in there and takes the shot, then lines up and does it again." — John Madden (former Raider coach, now Fox analyst)

Lesson 24

Star Power

"Look around close to home for role models" read the headline of a Deion Sanders column. "Neon Deion" (as he is known to his fans) played professional baseball (for the Braves) and professional football (for the Falcons) on the same day (in 1992). As a Cincinnati Red during the 1994 season, Sanders wrote a local newspaper column geared toward the youth of the community. He was also an important part of the 1995 Super Bowl 49er team.

In sharing his own role models, Sanders, says, "As a kid I admired many athletes for certain traits they displayed . . . and incorporated them into myself." The brashness and confidence of Muhammad Ali. The focus Hank Aaron had during his home-run chase despite all the controversy. The class and the respect Julius Erving commanded on and off the court. Even O.J. Simpson for going the extra mile for his teammates.

However, Sanders is quick to remind us these "weren't the people who instilled my morals and taught me right from wrong." He puts that responsibility on parents! "Kids put athletes on pedestals a little too much," says Sanders. "We really are just human."

We can look at players who are outstanding at their respective positions to learn how to play certain aspects of the game. Some of these players also contribute in meaningful ways to the communities where they live and play.

New York Jets quarterback Boomer Esiason has taken the offensive lead in fighting cystic fibrosis since his son, Gunnar, was diagnosed in March of 1993. *Sports Illustrated*'s cover story in October of that year shares Boomer's "crusade." While he may have personal motives for the CF battle, this type of commitment is not new to Esiason. Journalist Gary Smith reminds readers, "Few athletes anywhere gave as much time to charities as Boomer did — in a public way, raising $700,000 for the Arthritis Foundation and the Caring Program for Children, and in a private way, making frequent visits to kids with leukemia and cystic fibrosis at Children's Hospital," while with the Bengals in Cincinnati. He presented a $500,000 check toward the $1.6 million he has pledged to the Cystic Fibrosis Foundation in May of 1995. Esiason personally underwrites the salaries for the three-person staff of his Heroes Foundation that now has nearly 150 volunteers and over 200 corporate sponsors.

Boomer also takes a personal hands-on interest in Gunnar's fight. He performs the physical therapy massages on Gunnar whenever he is at home. Gunnar is lucky to have a real role model in his father — both on and off the field.

Another equally outstanding and generous NFL player is Reggie White. He and his wife built Hope Palace in Maryville, Tennessee, in 1991. It is a place for young pregnant-out-of-wedlock girls to find real love and compassion. They may stay after their babies are born until they can find a suitable permanent residence. The Whites hope to offer other Palaces around the country and are also working to establish a camp for young kids from inner-city gangs.

There are many other football players making similar impacts on the problems facing our society. Most go unheralded but should be commended for their love and service.

The real question is: What are **we** doing in our communities for the homeless, the unwed mothers, the youngsters in trouble with the law, and other social ills? Why not donate some time to help Habitat build a home for a needy family? Could you help with a Vacation Bible school in a slum area of your city? What kind of needs does your local Salvation Army currently face? Where can you help?

Christian service is not occasional heroic acts but a way of life done naturally every day. **We** are the "close-to-home role models" for our own children, their friends, and the kids in the neighborhood.

"For I am not seeking my own good but the good of many, so that they may be saved. Follow my example, as I follow the example of Christ" (1 Cor. 10:34; 11:1).

"A lot of people looking for role models in this world are often disappointed, but Reggie [White] never disappoints as a role model. He's someone you can hang your hat on." — John Spagnola (Philadelphia Eagle offensive lineman)

Lesson 25

Let's Celebrate

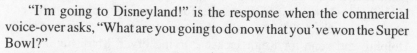

"I'm going to Disneyland!" is the response when the commercial voice-over asks, "What are you going to do now that you've won the Super Bowl?"

Breaking several records together during Super Bowl XXIX, 49er quarterback Steve Young and wide receiver Jerry Rice gave Disney a two-for-one ad. The tandem set not only personal records but led San Francisco as the first team to win all five Super Bowl appearances. Dallas has played in seven games but only won four. Pittsburgh has also won four. The Buffalo Bills hold the record for consecutive appearances (1991-94) but lost all four.

There are a myriad of ways that we celebrate athletic victories. John Madden once used his electronic marking pad to diagram the "wet hit" for television fans as members of one soon-to-be-victorious team maneuvered their way for the ceremonial "Gatorade bath" of the head coach. The president often phones "Congratulations!" to the Super Bowl Champions' locker room and may even invite the team to the White House. Hometown fans plan airport receptions, parades, and city-square celebrations.

Individual players have their own trademarks of jubilance. There was the "Ickey Shuffle" when the Bengals running back scored (until the NFL made such displays of "showmanship" illegal — assessing a penalty on the following kick-off). Players still point fingers into the crowd or express emotion in some way. Cowboy Michael Irvin takes off his helmet to salute the fans.

Some players use these moments of victory (whether personal or team) to express thanks to God for the talent He has given them. Some may point or use the sign of the cross as they look heavenward; others like Viking Cris Carter drop to their knees for a momentary prayer in the end zone. During the 1993-94 season, that was a common occurrence in the Dolphin end zone for Keith Jackson, Irving Fryar, Mark Ingram, and Keith Byars.

Now pro players huddle in what is known as the Circle of Prayer after each game. *Sports Spectrum* magazine reports that players from both teams kneel together at the 50-yard line. "For a while the TV cameras zoomed in. Now the ritual is ignored" by the press. "After Super Bowl XXIX, nearly two dozen players assembled at mid-field." Among them were Brent Jones, Charles Mann, and Steve Wallace from the 49ers and Junior Seau, John Carney, and Rodney Culver and Shawn Mitchell, the Charger chaplain for the last 10 years. All-Pro tackle Wallace led the audible prayer.

Do we celebrate with God? How do we share our joy with Him and others? In his book, *Laugh Again*, president of Dallas Theological Seminary, Chuck Swindoll says there is "no greater need today than the need for joy. Unexplainable, contagious, outrageous joy." He suggests joy is vital in that it brings "enthusiasm for life, determination to hang in there, and a strong desire to be of encouragement to others."

There is a distinct difference between happiness and joy. *Happiness* tends to depend on *happenings* or events. When things go well, we are happy; when they do not, we are sad. Inner joy transcends outward circumstances. Laughter can be a part of joy, but you can have joy without laughter. Joy is that attitude that allows us to realize that this life is only temporary, to find some humor in everything, and to live above our circumstances. It is an inner peace that even in the worst of situations, we can relax because we believe God is in control.

Win or lose, let's be joyful and thankful to God!

"Be joyful always; pray continually; give thanks in all circumstances, for this is God's will for you in Christ Jesus" (1 Thess. 5: 16-18).

"Thank You, Lord. I give You all the glory. I am only a vessel for You on earth." — Mark Ingram (Miami end zone, 12/5/94)

"Lord, we all want to live out our lives for You." — Steve Wallace (Circle of Prayer, Super Bowl XXIX, 1/29/95)

Lesson 26

Fumbles

Fans missed one of the most famous fumbles in football history. That is precisely why it's remembered. On November 17, 1968, with the score Jets 32 - Raiders 29, NBC cut from the game with 1:05 left to play in order to show the scheduled movie, *Heidi*. In the first 23 seconds of pre-emption, the Raiders scored a touchdown to take the lead. Then with 42 seconds remaining on the clock, they recovered a fumble on the kick-off and went on to score again. Final score: Raiders 43 - Jets 32 - NBC 0! The network execs had fumbled! Talk about irate fans!

The Buffalo Bills lost their fourth Super Bowl in a row (XXVIII) largely due to fumbles and other miscues. With the score tied in the first half, Cowboy reserve safety James Washington caused a fumble that Dallas recovered. A field goal put them ahead 6-3. Early in the second half, Cowboy teammate Leon Lett caused a fumble that Washington recovered and ran 46 yards for a TD. On the opening play of the fourth quarter, Washington also intercepted a pass, setting up the touchdown that locked the game for Dallas. He also had 11 solo tackles during the game.

Opponents don't always score on fumbles, but in some games they are the crucial plays that often change the momentum of a game.

We must be careful not to let Satan get a foothold through small, meaningless, or thoughtless acts. A single spark of gossip can turn into a forest fire of pain for the person being incriminated.

One drink may be all it takes to get a firm grip on someone who is an alcoholic

Just as in football, to avoid fumbles we must "hang on" to our faith. As we learn to rely on Jesus, His Word, and the Christian friends He brings into our lives, we can avoid many of the stumbling blocks of life that cause us to "let go" or "give up." Even if we do drop the ball once in a while, we must not be too embarrassed to again be involved in our church activities.

We can also be there for others to encourage them when they falter. We may need to recover the ball for them through forgiveness. Sometimes, we just need to "Be there!" as a part of their team.

What are you doing to encourage others to "hang onto their faith"?

"But encourage one another daily, as long as it is called Today, so that none of you may be hardened by sin's deceitfulness. We have come to share in Christ if we hold firmly till the end the confidence we had at first" (Heb. 3:13-14).

"After losing that one fumble, there was no way. You couldn't have gotten that ball away from me with a blowtorch." — Otto Graham, Cleveland QB, Hall of Fame, 1965 (after the 12/24/50 game when the Browns won NFL championship in their rookie season)

Lesson 27

Audible-Ready

Trailing with only 38 seconds on the game clock and one time-out left, Miami Dolphin quarterback Dan Marino set in behind his center. Making eye contact with Mark Ingram, his right-side receiver, Marino called out "Clock! Clock! Clock!" This play signaled the line to protect him so he could ground the ball to call the time-out. As normal for this call, he stepped back and looked toward the ground but suddenly fired a pass to Ingram who ran for the winning touchdown. The Jets defense had been duped. Miami won the game on a fake grounding!

Coach Don Shula credits the play to 1994 back-up QB Bernie Kosar. Not only had he brought the idea with him from Cleveland/Dallas, but he was the one who called the play to Marino on that specific down.

"It looked like improvising," says coach Don Shula, "but it was something we started to work into our two-minute drill that year."

Being "audible-ready" is one of Shula's secrets to success. It is his term for adaptability. In *Everyone's a Coach,* Shula defines audible: "An audible is a verbal command that tells our players to substitute new assignments for the ones they were prepared to perform."

"Audibles are not last-minute orders the quarterback has dreamed up out of nowhere." His own teammates would have no idea what was about to happen. Audibles are "strategies the players know about and have practiced."

If a quarterback dreams up some play that's never been practiced and quickly explains it to teammates in the huddle, that is not an audible. Audibles are called at the line of scrimmage to substitute for the play that has just been given in the huddle. The QB calls an audible when he sees the defense set in a formation that will read and kill the play just called. He will then call out a different play code that he feels will give the offense a better chance to move the ball.

Why stick with a game plan that isn't working? That is a valid question in every aspect of our lives — from business ventures that may be failing or at least stalled in their growth, to correcting our children if the current discipline isn't working.

"Audible-ready" in life means preparing to be adaptable and flexible. If our plans and schedules are so rigid and tightly set, any sudden mishap or interference can throw off our entire day (Jesus often chastized the Pharisees for their rigidity).

How many times have you heard the phrase "But we've **always** done it that way?" Tradition for tradition's sake is not always best. However, change for change's sake is not always correct either.

There are certain principles or convictions on which we should stand firm. How do we know which ones those are? Dave Holdren, Wesleyan pastor and former editor of curriculum for the denomination, says, "Convictions are so important that they should come primarily from the Word and the Holy Spirit and far less from another person's list." Holdren suggests that convictions are those essentials vital for our salvation. Who Christ is, why He died, and what we need to do to accept Him are the essentials.

Non-essentials may "fine-tune us as God's instruments" but we each may be called upon to play a different melody. Speaking in tongues, eating certain foods, dancing, going to movies, and other areas are individual concerns where we should not expect others to always agree with us. We all know faithful (faith-filled) Christians who feel differently about these areas, so they must not be essential to salvation.

Being audible-ready means being prepared — practicing these issues in our minds ahead of time, so we will know how to react when we reach the daily line of scrimmage. If a situation suddenly presents us where we are not audible-ready, we may need to use a time-out for prayer.

"For the kingdom of God is not a matter of eating and drinking, but of righteousness, peace and joy in the Holy Spirit" (Rom. 14:17).

"I want to be prepared with a plan — and then to expect the unexpected and be ready to change this plan . . . even to change at the last moment — as circumstances demand." — Don Shula (NFL coach with most wins)

Lesson 28

Sacked Again

"Sacking the quarterback" is the highlight of a defensive lineman's day. Just ask Reggie White or Derrick Thomas. In his career with the Eagles and Packers, White leads the NFL in career sacks with 137 (at the end of the 1994-95 season). Kansas City Chief Thomas has the most sacks in a single game with seven against the Seahawks in 1990.

If you want another perspective, ask the quarterbacks these two have sacked! While the sack may be the lineman's dream, it is the quarterback's nightmare.

Dallas Cowboy Troy Aikman has taken his share of sacks and hits. Clobbered by Dennis Brown in the 1993 playoff game with the 49ers, Aikman was knocked out. He recovered enough to watch "in a haze of confusion on the sidelines" but didn't remember anything about the game. However, even though he didn't "feel 100 percent during the practices," he returned to play the following week and went on to lead Dallas to their second straight Super Bowl.

One thing Aikman and other quarterbacks have learned — you have to get right back in the game after a sack. You can't concentrate on what went wrong; you must get ready for the next play or game. You must be persistent.

In his book, *Things Change*, Aikman shares that same attitude of perseverance in life. Written primarily for children, Aikman's book encourages kids to understand that whatever we face that may be scary (like the dark) or disappointing (like moving away from friends), each day offers new opportunities.

Starting life with a "mild form of club foot," Aikman was in tiny casts as an infant. Eventually his feet grew normally and he became a gifted athlete in several sports. He uses that example and others from his personal life to show that no matter what we are facing, things don't stay that way. "During dark days, keep focused and have faith and things will change," shares Aikman.

Sometimes it's just a matter of waiting until we better understand what's going on. Aikman shares about his fear of death after his grandfather died, the loneliness of moving from California to Oklahoma during junior high, and other typical traumas of youth. He shares how he found success in each of these situations and says we, too, can be "champions over change"— winning even through losses.

What kind of fears do you face now? What trauma has hit your life? Perhaps it's a new job or the commitment of marriage. Maybe fatherhood has just arrived (or is on the horizon). Do you feel trapped in a mid-life crisis or by the responsibility of aging parents? What can you do?

Adapting to change and persistence like Aikman shares in his book to the kids are vital. "Perseverance means to continue doing something in the face of difficulty and opposition — to be steadfast in purpose — to persist." It is often the persistent, though disadvantaged, person who wins the race. Remember the story of *The Tortoise and the Hare*?

"Hang in there! is more than an expression to someone experiencing hardship or difficulty; it is sound advice for anyone intent on doing good in the world." So says William Bennett, former education secretary and drug czar for Presidents Reagan and Bush. He also warns that we can be persistently wrong, so we need intelligence and a practical understanding of issues. Seek understanding and wisdom from God and other people of virtue.

"Perseverance is an essential quality of character in high-level leadership," says Bennett. "Much good that might have been achieved in the world is lost through hesitation, faltering, wavering, vacillating, or just not sticking to it."

So whatever you are facing, just persevere!

"But we also rejoice in our sufferings, because we know that suffering produces perseverance; perseverance, character; and character, hope" (Rom. 5:3).

"By the time I'm climbing back up from going down, I'm already thinking about the next play." — Joe Namath (QB, Hall of Fame, 1985)

Lesson 29
Football Is Football . . .

. . . is football is football. Just as there is a variety of roses, football is not always the same. Fans will argue about whether the AFC or the NFC has the best teams. Other fans debate which colleges play in tougher conferences. The Pac-Ten? The Big Ten? The Big Eight? Some of the best teams may be independent like Notre Dame and Florida State.

Scoring, rules, and even the field may be different depending where you watch the game. The yard lines and hash marks forming the gridiron pattern of the field vary from high school to college to the professional level. Hash marks are closer to the sidelines in high school. The distance between the uprights of the goalpost is wider for high school (23' 4") than for college or pro (18' 6") kickers trying for field goals and conversions.

Football varies even more in Canada. Not only is the field larger, but they play with 12 men (per team) on the field and have only three downs instead of four like we are used to in the United States. Some players made names for themselves in the CFL between college and the NFL. Joe Theismann played several years with Toronto, and Warren Moon led the Edmonton team to five Grey Cup championships (the Canadian equivalent of our Super Bowl).

Another version of football began in 1986. Called Arena Football, it is played with only eight players per team on a smaller indoor field (hockey or basketball arenas with padded walls surrounding the playing area).

Football "purists" watch **only** the NFL, but they cannot keep advocates of the other versions of the game from enjoying college, CFL, and Arena games.

Similar religious "purists" believe their denomination or local church is the "one and only way to God."

Fortunately, there are strong ecumenical movements that not only counter these extremely dogmatic groups but who truly promote Christ's "love one another as I have loved you" teaching. They look for the Bible-based truths to share rather than disagreeing on the non-essential issues.

Well-known and beloved evangelist Billy Graham says, "God loves homosexuals as much as anyone else. I think homosexuality is a sin, but no greater than idolatry or adultery. In my judgment, it's not that big." He looks beyond the sin in order to love the sinner and bring him/her back to a loving relationship with Christ. "There is a great division in the religious community today," says Graham, "I preach to unite people."

The ever-growing Promise Keeper movement shares this theme of unity as one of its goals: "A Promise Keeper is committed to reaching beyond any racial and denominational barriers to demonstrate the power of biblical unity. We can demonstrate that what history, the political process, and the legal system could not do, faith, obedience, repentance, and unity in Jesus Christ can do. . . . The body of Christ is called to a higher standard — not mere tolerance, but love such as Christ has for you" (from *Seven Promises* section by Phillip Porter and Gordon England).

They suggest "building relationships" that cross racial and cultural lines. Look for examples where we may have already found this unity. Playing sports, serving in the military, working on the job, or joining a college fraternity often have provided these experiences for many people.

If those who cheer each week for teams composed of inter-racial players would only work together half as well in their personal lives, we could eliminate much of the hostility in society today.

There is a great difference between unity and uniformity. We are not called to be alike, but we are called to be united.

"Make every effort to keep the unity of the Spirit through the bond of peace. There is one body and one Spirit — just as you were called to one hope ... one Lord, one faith, one baptism: one God and Father who is over all and through all and in all" (Eph. 4:3-5).

"Professional football players have had more experience and ... are practically all stars from end to end and ... play a technically more perfect game. On the other hand, the college game brings out something which is lacking in the pro game — I guess you could call it spirit." — Jim Thorpe (charter member Pro Football Hall of Fame, 1963)

Lesson 30

Retirement

While the sun was bright on April 18, 1995, in San Francisco, 49er fans found it a dark and gloomy day. Joe Montana was announcing his retirement from professional football.

Montana not only led the 49ers to four Super Bowls but was MVP in three of them, setting numerous records. He also won two season MVPs.

Montana said he was leaving with "No regrets. Sixteen years [two with Kansas City] and the things we accomplished as a team. There's nothing more I could ask for." His wife Jennifer says, "Once he makes up his mind, Joe doesn't look back."

Montana has already invested in an Indy Car team. He enjoys golf and piloting his own single-engine plane and hopes to add a vineyard to some property he is developing in the Napa Valley area.

He will also follow other former players (and coaches) into broadcasting. Frank Gifford, Terry Bradshaw, Joe Theismann, Ahmad Rashad, John Madden, Mike Ditka — the list is endless.

Merlin Olsen combined broadcasting and acting. Working with the late Michael Landon on *Little House on the Prairie*, Olsen was later given his own series, *Father Murphy*.

Rosey Grier appeared on *Kojak*, among other TV shows, but is best known for media coverage.

Former Buffalo Bill quarterback Jack Kemp (most AFL

Joe Montana
Notre Dame University

passing yards in the sixties) became a U.S. congressman from Buffalo, and later served in the White House cabinet in the eighties.

We all need to plan for the future — not just financially but emotionally as well. Develop hobbies that can last a lifetime. Golf, sailing, bowling, tennis, walking, and other athletic endeavors also benefit our health. What about other activities like serving on a short-term project with our church mission office?

Some of us fear having to give up these activities as our physical prowess lessens. How much strength does it take to lead a Bible study or to give a hug to a lonely child? There are young families in nearly every neighborhood or church who do not have any "grandparents" nearby. Attend the children's ball games. Let the kids read to you!

In his book, *No Wrinkles On the Soul*, Richard L. Morgan says, "The word *retirement* can be misleading. For some, retirement connotes a stop sign or a rocking chair. Perhaps the word *redirection* is a better one." He challenges us to change our lifestyle and find new priorities. Morgan says, "We may *do* a bit less so that we can *be* who we are."

"Be all you can be!"

"Even when I am old and gray, do not forsake me, O God, till I declare your power to the next generation, your might to all who are to come" (Ps. 71:18).

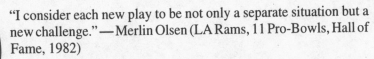

"I consider each new play to be not only a separate situation but a new challenge." — Merlin Olsen (LA Rams, 11 Pro-Bowls, Hall of Fame, 1982)

Sources & Recommended Reading

In accordance with copyright laws, all quotes are brief enough in nature and not in competition with any of the following texts and sources that written permission was not necessary. However, we do wish to acknowledge these authors and individuals and encourage you to purchase the books for further reading.

Aikman, Troy with Greg Brown, *Things Change* (Dallas, TX: Taylor Publishing, 1995).

Bass, Tom, *Play Football the NFL Way* (New York, NY: St. Martin's Press, 1990).

Bennett, William, editor, *The Book of Virtues* (New York, NY: Simon & Schuster, 1993).

Carter, Craig, editor, *The Sporting News Pro Football Guide, Almanac of the 1993 Season* (St. Louis, MO: The Sporting News Publishing Co., Times Mirror Company, 1994 edition).

Chad, Norman, "Super Bowl Spectacular," *TV Guide*, 1/28/95.

Daly, Dan and Bob O'Donnell, *The Pro Football Chronicle* (New York, NY: Collier/Macmillan Publishing, 1990).

DeLuca, Sam, *Football Made Easy* (Middle Village, NY: Jonathan David Publishers, Inc., 1983).

Dieter, Melvin E., "Wolves in Shepherds' Clothing," *Adult Teacher*, The Enduring Word Series, Wesleyan Publishing House, Indianapolis, IN, Fall 1984.

Encarta (CD-rom). Microsoft, 1995.

"40 Pictures to Remember," *Sports Illustrated*, 11/14/94.

Foster, Richard, *Celebration of Discipline* (New York, NY: Harper & Row, Publishers, 1978).

Gaither, Gloria, *What My Parents Did Right* (Nashville, TN: Star Song Publishing, 1991).

Garrity, John, "And down the road . . ." *Sports Illustrated*, 11/22/93.

Herbst, Dan, editor, *The Art of Place-Kicking and Punting* (New York, NY: Linden Press, Mountain Lion Books, 1985).

Hoffer, Richard, "Forrest Grier," *Sports Illustrated*, 3/20/95.

Hoffer, Richard and Shelley Smith, "Putting His House in Order," *Sports Illustrated*, 1/16/95.

Holdren, Dave, "Life Long Learning — Convictions: Who needs them?" *Emphasis* (Indianapolis, IN: Wesleyan Press, 1984).

Hutchcraft, Ron, "Huddle Time," *Partnership Magazine* Christianity Today, July/August 1985.

Ingle, Matthew, "DePauw, Class of '96," *Sports Illustrated*, 11/22/93.

Jenkins, Sally, "The Mouth That Roars," *Sports Illustrated,* 10/25/93.

Johnson, Otto, editor, *Information Please Almanac* (Boston, MA: Houghton Mifflin, Co., 1995).

Keeney, John, "Justifying Grace" talk, Greater Dayton En. ~us Women's Walk #21, February 1995.

King, Peter, "Forty for the Ages: #4 — Jim Brown," *Sports Illustrated*, (Anniversary Issue), 9/19/94.

King, Peter, "Inside the NFL — Weekend at Bernie's," *Sports Illustrated,* 11/22/93.

King, Peter, "QB or not QB?" *Sports Illustrated*, 7/27/92.

Layden, Tim, "The Lion King," *Sports Illustrated*, 12/26/94.

Lieber, Jill, "Never Back Down," *Sports Illustrated*, 9/7/92.

MacDonald, Mark; Kevin Brown; and Ray Mitsch, *Setting New Boundaries (Daily Devotions for Those in Recovery)* (Nashville, TN: Thomas Nelson Publishers, 1991).

Madden, John with Dave Anderson, *One Knee Equals Two Feet (And Everything Else You Need to Know About Football)* (New York, NY: Villard Books, 1986).

Meserole, Mike, editor, *The 1992 Information Please Sports Almana* (Boston, MA: Houghton Mifflin Company, 1991).

The Methodist Hymnal (Nashville, TN: The United Methodist Publishing House, 1964).

Miller, J. David, *The Super Bowl Book of Football, Sports Illustrated for Kids* (Boston, MA: The Time, Inc., Magazine Company, 1990).

Minirth, Frank, *You Can!* (Nashville, TN: Thomas Nelson Publishers, 1994).

Montville, Leigh, "NFL — Forward Progress," *Sports Illustrated*, 9/5/94.

Morgan, Richard L, *No Wrinkles On The Soul* (Nashville, TN: Upper Room Books, 1990).

Nack, William, "Tell It Like It Is," *Sports Illustrated*, 5/1/95.

Neff, Beers, Barton, Taylor, Veerman, and Galvin, editors, *Practical Christianity* (Wheaton, IL: Tyndale House Publishers, Inc., 1987),"What It Means to Repent" by Charles Colson; "Sharing Our Faith — Witnessing" by Jay Kesler; "Two Kinds of Pride" by Jay Kesler; "How Does a Person Become a Christian?" by Luis Palau.

1995 National College Cheerleading Championship, ESPN, Bristol, CN, 6/10/95.

1995 National High School Cheerleading Championship, ESPN, Bristol, CN, 7/2/95.

Oates, Bob, *The Winner's Edge* (New York, NY: Mayflower Books, 1980).

O'Brien, Michael, *VINCE* (New York, NY: William Morrow & Company, Inc., 1987).

"Open Court - No Sunday Sports?" *Sports Spectrum*, April 1995.

"Perseverance" talk, The Walk to Emmaus, *The Upper Room*, Nashville, TN

"Pros At Prayer" in "Waddy's World," *Sports Spectrum*, April 1995.

Puro, George and Kyle Veltrop, *The Sporting News Pro Football Register* (St. Louis, MO: The Sporting News Publishing Co., Times Mirror Company, 1994 edition).

Rambeck, Richard, *Detroit Lions* (Mankato, MN: Creative Education, Inc., 1991).

Range, Peter Ross, "Billy Graham on TV, Religion, and More," *TV Guide*, 8/6/94.

Range, Peter Ross, "God & The News — Why Is This Woman the Only Religion Reporter on TV?" *TV Guide*, 8/6/94.

Raspberry, William, "Why Men Won't Go to Church," *Cincinnati Enquirer*, Cincinnati, OH, 6/5/95.

"The Redskin Resolution" and "President's Decision,"*Miamian* (alumni magazine), Miami University, Oxford, OH, Winter 1993-94.

Rosberg, Gary, Ph.D., "Choosing to Love Again," *Focus on the Family Magazine*, October 1992.

Sanders, Deion, "On the Line with Prime," *Cincinnati Enquirer*, Cincinnati, OH, 8/7/94.

Schoor, Gene, *100 Years of Notre Dame Football* (New York, NY: William Morrow and Company, Inc., 1987).

Schuller, Robert, *Be-(Happy) Attitudes* (Waco, TX: Word Books, 1985).

Seamands, David A., *If Only* (Wheaton, IL: Victor Books, 1995).

Seven Promises of a Promise Keeper (Colorado Springs, CO: Focus on the Family Publishing, 1994).

Shula, Don and Ken Blanchard, *Everyone's a Coach* (Grand Rapids, MI: Zondervan Publishing, 1995).

Silver, Michael, "All Hail the King," *Sports Illustrated*, 4/24/95.

Simms, Phil with Vinny Ditrani, "A Giant Step," *Sports Illustrated*, 1/23/95.

Singletary, Mike with Jerry Jenkins, *Singletary on Singletary* (Nashville, TN: Thomas Nelson Publishers, 1991).

Smith, Gary, "We're Going to Beat This Thing," *Sports Illustrated*, 10/4/93.

Strand, Robert, *Moments for Fathers* (Green Forest, AR: New Leaf Press, Inc., 1993).

Strother, Shelby, *NFL Top 40 — The Greatest Pro Football Games of All Time* (New York, NY: Viking Penguin Inc., 1988).

Sullivan, Tim, "Boomer's Blitz Against CF Is Effective," *Cincinnati Enquirer,* Cincinnati, OH, 5/18/95.

Swindoll, Charles R., *Laugh Again* (Dallas, TX: Word Publishing, 1991).

Telander, Rick, "The Defense Never Rests," *Sports Illustrated,* 12/13/93.

Telander, Rick, "The Last Angry Men," *Sports Illustrated*, 9/6/93.

Telander, Rick, "Superb," *Sports Illustrated*, 2/6/95.

Thomas, Cal; "Good and Evil Are Clear Now," *Cincinnati Enquirer,* Cincinnati, OH, 4/26/95.

Thomas, Dave, *Well Done!* (Grand Rapids, MI: Zondervan Publishing, 1994).

Vilardo, Michael, Trinity United Methodist Church, Milford, Ohio, 1994 sermon.

Waitley, Denis, *The Double Win* (Old Tappan, NJ: Fleming H. Revell Company, 1985).

The Walk to Emmaus, *The Upper Room* (taken from "Study" talk, Greater Cincinnati Women's Walk #42), July 1991.

White, Reggie with Terry Hill, *Reggie White — Minister of Defense* (Brentwood, TN: Wolgemuth & Hyatt Publishers, Inc., 1991).

White, Reggie and Larry Reid, *The Reggie White Touch Football Playbook* (Warrenton, VA: Warrenton Press, 1992).

Whiteside, Kelly, "AFC east," *Sports Illustrated,* 9/5/94.

Whitman, Robert L., *Jim Thorpe and the Oorang Indians* (Defiance, OH: The Hubbard Company, 1984).

The World Book Encyclopedia, vol. 7-F and 21-W (Chicago, IL: World Book, Inc., 1983).

Young, Mark, editor, *The Guinness Book of Sports Records 1994-95, Facts on File* (New York, NY: Guinness Publishing Ltd., 1994).

Zimmerman, Paul, "Armed Forces," *Sports Illustrated,* 10/25/93.

Zimmerman, Paul, "Don't Cross This Line," *Sports Illustrated,* 9/5/94.

Zimmerman, Paul, "The Fumble," *Sports Illustrated,* 2/7/94.